T0079722

LOBSTER

Edible

Series Editor: Andrew F. Smith

EDIBLE is a revolutionary new series of books dedicated to food and drink that explores the rich history of cuisine. Each book reveals the global history and culture of one type of food or beverage.

Already published

Lobster

A Global History

Elisabeth Townsend

REAKTION BOOKS

To Jeff with love and gratitude

Published by Reaktion Books Ltd
33 Great Sutton Street
London EC1V 0DX, UK
www.reaktionbooks.co.uk

First published 2011

Printed and bound in China by C&C Offset Printing Co. Ltd

British Library Cataloguing in Publication Data
Townsend, Elisabeth.
Lobster: a global history. – (Edible)
1. Lobsters. 2. Lobster fisheries – History.
3. Cooking (Lobsters)
4. Cooking (Lobsters) – History.
I. Title II. Series
641.3 95-DC22

ISBN: 978 1 86189 794 7

Contents

Introduction:
What is a Lobster?

The world's love affair with lobster began out of necessity. It wasn't a mutual affection though: it was as lopsided as unrequited love. Humans needed to eat and the crustacean was often within easy reach by hand, spear, long hook, baskets and later nets and traps. But the shellfish eventually became more than just grub – its status shifted from vital protein to pauper's food to cultural icon.

This relationship has always been complex. When lobsters were abundant many coastal dwellers disdained them. But their popularity with wealthy urban diners drove innovations that nearly annihilated the stocks. It was through these innovations and mass marketing that lobster ended up on dinner plates in Tokyo, Japan and Dubuque, Iowa. Clearly, this affair d'amour isn't a tawdry fling. It's a long-term relationship.

The worldwide lobster industry is still thriving because early regulations prevented overfishing. Yet worry about losing the species continues amid record catches and several perplexing scares, and today lobsters and their consumers are under another threat. As concern about the humane treatment of lobsters heats up, demand may decline as purveyors become reluctant to sell them. Compassion is building for all

Salvador Dalí, *Lobster Telephone*, 1936. The lobster is an icon that has appeared in many works of art, including this example by the famous Spanish surrealist.

animals and that includes the lobster. Some countries are considering broadening animal welfare laws to include these lively shellfish. Once again new technology is a significant factor – with new killing machines that use electrocution and water pressure. Divorced from the primal experience of killing our dinner, we are in danger of losing the connection between the food we ingest and its origin. The idyllic experience of eating a freshly boiled lobster on a coastal dock may become extinct. If that happens, will anyone recognize the feisty iconic shellfish on Salvador Dalí's *Lobster Telephone* or on Maine's licence plate? Will we even remember what lobsters symbolize – summertime leisure on the rockbound coast, eating exquisite seafood with friends provided by independent fisherwomen and men braving the elements to bring in the catch? What happens to the experience of 'eating a lobster'?

Humans and lobsters have a long history together. Long before we knew much about this crustacean, lobsters found their way into artistic creations as a revered shellfish, symbol, status or otherwise. Spiny lobsters adorn a fifteenth-century BC Egyptian temple in an aquatic scene depicting new, fascinating animals and plants from an expedition down the Red Sea along the coast of East Africa. As early as the first century BC, spiny lobsters appeared in a mosaic floor in the dining room of ancient Pompeii and in Virgil's *Aeneid*, as Palinurus, the helmsman of the Trojan fleet. They are part of a mosaic floor in the dining room of a Pompeian house depicting how the floor would look after the diners had finished – leaving the inedible shells and bones 'dropped under the tables'.

Lobsters adorn everything from Maine licence plates to fine art, literature and movies.

This rare, polka-dotted lobster was found near Rockport, Maine in 2004. *Homarus* lobsters come in many colours besides their typical greenish brown or blackish blue.

Humans are still captivated by lobster. But most lobster lovers know less about them than some of the early Egyptians or Peruvians or Italians. To begin our introduction to the fascinating history of lobsters and their consumption, meet Fiona. She is dressed in a spotted orange and yellow outfit. At seven years old, she weighs a pound and three-quarters (800 g). And because of her spiffy get-up, she is about as unusual as say one in 30 million. This youngster, probably a yellow lobster in spite of her orange spots, was caught in Canada near Prince Edward Island in 2009. Instead of being sold as a lobster dinner, she lives in a tank with close to 100 other lobsters in Arnold's Lobster and Clam Bar in Eastham, Massachusetts and may be donated to an aquarium. She was named for owner Nathan Nickerson's girlfriend's granddaughter. How Fiona survived is still a mystery. Usually lobsters in the Atlantic Ocean are a greenish brown or a blackish blue so they blend into their habitat. Fiona is the product of a rare genetic mutation, and would be an easy target for predators in her yellow shell, as are the scarce royal blue, red, white and even two-toned lobsters. 'All of these except the white ones turn red when cooked', as do lobsters worldwide, writes Dr Robert Bayer, an American lobster researcher. But she does have two powerful weapons to defend herself – her claws.

Fiona is one of two distinct varieties of lobsters – clawed and clawless – that are worthy of any food lover's attention and commercially important. In Fiona's family there are three noteworthy clawed lobsters. She is the American in a group of European and Norway lobsters that are found in the colder, northern Atlantic Ocean. But she is not the only beauty. The clawless group comprises the sometimes stunning, ubiquitous

The brilliant blue spiny lobster is just one example of the widespread and varied clawless lobsters found mostly in warmer waters.

spiny lobsters of warmer, tropical waters primarily in Australasia, plus their cousins, the slipper lobsters and furry lobsters.

What do they have in common? All lobsters are treasured for their 'firm, sweet white meat', which is 'satisfyingly full of flavour and . . . remarkably similar the world over', said British chef Rick Stein, who advocates eating lobster where they come right out of the ocean. All are sold live, as frozen tails or cooked, and have ten legs on the underside, as they are in the decapod family.

Mostly nocturnal and dwelling on the ocean floor, lobsters eat what's available in their environment but prefer crustaceans, fish, molluscs, sea urchins, snails and worms. For a primitive creature, clawed lobsters are more finicky than we realize, preferring fresh food – they like a variety of select plants and almost 100 different animals including lobster bait (salted or fresh fish bits). Sometimes clawed lobsters in captivity in tanks turn to cannibalism, though this has not been seen in the wild. If necessary, both lobster species may forage for dead animals. While fish gobble their food whole, these crustaceans are 'nibblers'. They 'pull, tear, crush and manipulate food items' until they're bite-size pieces that fit into their mouths. Both lobsters migrate annually from warmer, shallower waters to deeper heat-stable waters in winter.

Clawed and clawless lobsters have a common ancestor from about 251 to 290 million years ago. Yet despite their similarities, they're not close relatives. Clawed lobsters are more closely related to freshwater crayfish than to the clawless group. But which should you eat?

The Clawed Lobsters

The American, the European and the Norwegian clawed lobsters are only three out of over thirty in the Nephropidae family that lobster devotees covet. The primary species of true clawed lobsters are the European *Homarus gammarus* and its slightly larger cousin, the American *H. americanus*. These two shellfish probably are called 'true' to distinguish them from crayfish, with which they were grouped in Aristotle's time. Their names have mutated as scientists learned more about the different kinds of lobsters and as language changed. Most likely 'lobster' came from old English *lobystre*, possibly evolving from the Latin *locusta* or locust. In 1837 the naturalist Milne Edwards wisely bunched lobsters in a specific genus with the Latin *Homarus*.

If you're imagining enormous meaty claws, that's the American lobster. Some say it has become the world's gold standard. The first pair of claws gets your attention, but they have smaller ones on the next two pairs of legs too. These renowned and sought-after crustaceans inhabit cold salt water from Labrador to North Carolina. They are solitary and aggressive, sometimes eating their partner after mating. The

An old engraving shows the primitive clawed or *Homarus* lobster that is typically found in the colder waters of the North Atlantic.

Enormous claws, especially those of the American lobsters, provide
a powerful defence against predators such as fish and are coveted by
consumers. As seen here, the underside of a live lobster can be orange.

Gulf of Maine has been hospitable to the American lobster,
nicknamed the Maine lobster, as has the Gulf of St Lawrence.
Both support the two biggest hauling countries: Canada and
the US.

Usually marketed live, diners will see lobsters as a subtle,
mottled bluish black or greenish brown colour in tanks
before they turn bright orange-red when cooked, hence the
moniker 'the cardinal of the seas'. Habitat influences the
colour of the live lobster but the change to red after cooking
is a result of a pigment in its carapace (body shell, or exoskeleton) that covers the head and thorax of this crustacean.

Today's consumer will most likely enjoy an American lobster that is less than 1 kg (1–1.5 lb, on average) in weight, when
caught in shallow water. Some say large lobsters are as flavour-
ful as smaller ones. However, few of us will ever try the larger

ones that grow to 20+ kilograms (45+ lb) and almost 2 metres (5–6 ft) long (common before the mid-1800s) during their lives of 50 to perhaps more than 100 years. The largest Atlantic lobster caught in Nova Scotia, Canada was about 20 kg (45 lb), according to the *Guinness World Records*. Another from the waters off the Virginia coast, in the 1930s, was over a metre (39 in.) long and almost 20 kg (45 lb).

European lobsters are a long-standing emblem of luxury, much like champagne and caviar for Europeans. Consequently they were in short supply well before the American lobster was in jeopardy. The dark blue European shellfish lives on the rocky bottoms of waters from Norway down to the

This New York dockworker displays rare giant lobster claws from 1943 at the Fulton fish market.

While the European lobster or *Homarus gammarus* may not always have the typical dark blue shell, it is still a symbol of luxury. A lobster uses its claws to rip food into bite-size pieces, which it stuffs into its mouth using the small claws on the walking legs.

Mediterranean Sea. On average, it is about 30 centimetres (12 in.) long and weighs 300–500 grams (11–18 oz). It can grow to almost 75 cm (2.5 ft), with northern lobsters reaching 1–1.5 kg (2¼–3¼ lb).

The slender, pale pink Norway lobster (*Nephrops norvegicus*), ranging in length from 15–25 cm (6–10 in.), is very popular too. It resembles, but is not, a freshwater crayfish. The most colourful of the Atlantic lobsters, it also can be a rose or orange-red colour, with red and white bands on the claws. Found in the Atlantic from Iceland to Morocco, it's sold fresh, with bright black eyes and shiny pink shells, cooked

Norway lobsters, less expensive than European lobsters, have a shrimp-like flavour.

or frozen. Usually only the tail is eaten since the claws and body are so petite. Norway lobster goes by enough names to be confusing for seafood lovers. The French call them langoustines, as well as *demoiselles de Cherbourg*. When caught fresh from the Irish Sea, they are called Dublin Bay prawns, simply because they were sold off boats coming into Dublin Bay. Its diminutive is lobsterette. Dubbed Italian scampi also when fished in Adriatic waters, Venetians boil or fry them in oil and serve them with garlic sauce. Nearly a standard on British menus, scampi are steamed and, like their larger cousins, are dipped in a butter, salt and lemon juice mixture. They may be brushed with olive oil and grilled, used in paella, poached and served whole, or served in European interpretations of Chinese and Vietnamese dishes. With a shrimp-like flavour that is more pronounced after they have been frozen, they appear in prawn cocktails, perhaps fried, curried or in cream sauce.

The Clawless Lobsters

'Home is where the spiny lobsters are', brags a resort ad for tropical Turks and Caicos Islands in the West Indies. These clawless lobsters are also at home in rock crevices and dangerous coral reefs in warmer Asian and Australasian waters, hence the pet name rock lobster. Without large defensive claws, they use their brilliant spiny shell as armour. (While they have no claws like the Atlantic lobster, the female spiny lobster has a small one on the fifth pair of legs.) Probably to scare off predators, most spiny lobsters manipulate their two enormously long spiky antennae, rubbing them against their exoskeleton making a screeching sound much like a beginning violinist. That's why the French call it *langouste* (Latin for locust, *locusta*). It's also known as Cape lobster, cave lobster, crawfish and sea crayfish. It is not a crayfish, which is a freshwater crustacean.

Fiona may be pretty, but spiny lobsters are lookers too and may be smarter. The Caribbean spiny lobster (*Panulirus argus*) appears 'to use the earth's magnetic field as a compass', becoming the first backboneless animal to have homing abilities. These lobsters are famous for their autumnal migrations and now we know how they do it. Some researchers at the

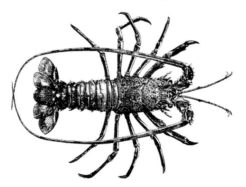

Spiny lobsters such as the one depicted in this old engraving have been used as a food source for at least 40,000 years.

University of North Carolina wanted to know if they could identify their position even when they were moved to a completely new area. After approximately 100 lobsters were transferred to an unfamiliar location in covered containers via roundabout routes, it became apparent that they knew where they were on the earth. Even with their eyes masked in the new spot, the lobsters turned toward their capture location, about 12–37 kilometres (7.5–23 miles) away, and started for home. The same scientists, Larry C. Boles and Kenneth J. Lohmann, had previously discovered that the spiny lobsters already had one component of navigation – an internal magnetic compass. The Caribbean spiny lobsters join an elite group of animals with true navigation capabilities including butterflies, birds such as geese and homing pigeons, salmon and whales.

In the autumn, the Caribbean and Florida spiny lobsters (*Panulirus argus*) relocate to deeper water, moving in single file in groups of around sixty. About 100,000 lobsters migrate in this fashion to evade the autumn storms that produce waves on the coast. Their spear-like antennae come in handy for another reason: they use them when travelling to stay connected to their companions, resting them on the lobster in front of them. It's a lobster conga line, snaking across the floor of the Caribbean.

Safer in groups, they will stand their ground and fight, striking with their long antennae. When not migrating, spiny lobsters like to hide in sunken ships that provide dark places safe during the day from predators, and then come out at night to forage. Spiny lobsters are much more social than American lobsters, and readily share crevices, holes, rock ledges or edges of vegetation with others of their species.

But the spiny lobster's unusual ability to defend itself has not prevented it from becoming one of the world's most

.red and highly esteemed seafoods. Demand has in-
..ased over recent decades so that these crustaceans are cap-
..ured and sold in more than 90 countries. Some say that the
largest spiny lobster was three feet long and weighed almost
12 kg (over 26 lb). They estimate that this crustacean might
live to be 25–50 years old. Out of roughly 45 species in the
spiny lobster or Palinuridae family, a handful are commercially important and a few more are precious to connoisseurs.
Given that many have adapted to different environments and
they are caught widely, consumers will discover spiny lobsters
on menus that go beyond this starter checklist.

The spiny lobster *Palinurus elephas* is found from England's southern tip to the Mediterranean though most live in
tropical waters. It has other monikers: European, common,
Mediterranean and red lobster.

On the Pacific coast of America, gourmands esteem the
California spiny lobster, *P. interruptus*, from Pacific waters,

The social spiny lobsters willingly share coral reefs and rock ledges when
hiding in the daytime, like these Australian *Panulirus cygnus*, and will fight in
groups using their long antennae as weapons. Like all lobsters, they forage
at night. (Shark Bay, Western Australia, 1993.)

Hiroshige Andō, *Lobster and Shrimps*, 1835–44, print. The spiny lobster has been a delicacy in the Japanese diet for centuries.

known as langosta. Also in American waters is the West Indian spiny lobster, *P. argus*, found from Bermuda to Brazil, and rarely in the Atlantic as far north as North Carolina. In Asia, two noteworthy lobsters are the ornate rock lobster, *P. ornatus*, and the painted spiny lobster, *P. versicolor*. Rock lobster fisheries are profitable in New Zealand (rock lobster or crayfish, *Jasus edwardsii*), Australia (western rock lobster or western crayfish, *P. cygnus*) and South Africa (rock lobster, *J. lalandii*). The largest rock lobster fishery in the world started in Australia after Europeans arrived in the late 1800s.

Live spiny lobsters fetch some of the highest prices – especially among the Japanese, whose native species include *P. japonicus* – but most tails are marketed frozen. Today they are on menus from Japan to Europe, and are especially popular on the European continent. The French, particularly Parisians, enjoy them so much that imports from South America and North Africa augment the meagre local supply.

Only the tail of the clawless slipper lobster is eaten. This species (*Scyllarides haanii*) uses its flat head like a shovel for digging and is found in local markets in the Indo-Pacific.

Prepared in the same manner as true lobster, the meat is shipped worldwide. Americans import millions of pounds from Australia, New Zealand, Mexico, South Africa and South America.

Spiny lobsters are treasured for their meat, which comes from their abdomens but is marketed as the tail. The 'dense, rather coarse and white' meat has been described as 'flavour-ful, but . . . less pronounced . . . than that of the true lobster' opined an anonymous writer, but 'make just as good eating' according to Stein. These distant relatives of true lobster can be prepared in similar ways, though he cautions that they have 'a tendency to dryness'.

Called bugs or bay lobsters in the western Pacific, the Moreton Bay bug and Balmain bug are the most popular slipper lobsters, sometimes called shovel-nosed or Spanish lobsters (two of over 50 species in the Scyllaridae family). This wide-ranging species is also found in the Mediterranean,

and off both Scottish and Hawaiian waters. The slipper lobster is an additional edible crustacean to be fished from
tropical oceans and seas, even if it has little economic impor-
tance. The cousin of spiny and furry lobsters, it too is not a
true lobster. Its distinguishing characteristics are large, plate-
like antennae protruding from the head, besides being
clawless and somewhat flat. The Moreton Bay bug (*Thenus ori-
entalis*) is well known in Australasia. Considered a versatile
delicacy in Queensland restaurants, it is served in both sweet
and savoury dishes. It swims in Moreton Bay, after which it
is named, plus the Indian Ocean, and even the western edge
of the Pacific Ocean. In Europe, it is also called the *cigale de
mer* (cricket of the sea) from the snapping, cricket-like noise
they make underwater. The Balmain bug (*Ibacus peronii*), from
Balmain, New South Wales, is pincerless, and employs its
short, wide antennae for digging through sand and mud off
Australia's coast. It is commonly found in Sydney fish markets and shops. It is also found 'from the Red Sea and east
coast of Africa eastwards to India, China, southern Japan,
[and] the Philippines' wrote Alan Davidson, author of many
seafood guides. None of the furry lobsters (Synaxidae family), 'covered in short hair', are commercially important.

Lobsters go by many names and come in many colours.
But regardless of the name or colour, all lobsters are edible.
And whether plucked from the ocean or purchased in fish
markets, lobsters have been a fascinating part of human history for thousands of years.

I

From Fertilizer to the Dinner Table

Lobsters were here and we were eating them long before anyone knew the difference between the more than one hundred varieties. The evidence is in the shells. They have existed for over 250 million years, with remnants found in Europe and the Americas. The 110-million-year-old relic of a spiny lobster was discovered in 1995 in Chiapas, Mexico. In New York's Long Island Sound, fossils show that the American lobster has looked like an armour-plated cockroach for about a hundred million years. Well-preserved remains form a lobster bed in the 146-million-year-old Greensand formation that was unearthed on an island off the coast of southern England. In Bavaria, shell fossils date from almost 200 million years ago. Lobster shells, preserved as fossils, are a sign of their role in our lives before we started keeping written records.

Shells are also traces of what prehistoric people ate globally. Our ancestors were wildly enthusiastic about shellfish, if the middens – or shell mounds found in fishing communities – are any indication. Large heaps of shells on British shores prove the popularity of shellfish with prehistoric seaside communities. Piles are also found both in South Africa, dating from about 100,000 years ago, and in Australia and Papua New Guinea, from close to 35,000 years ago. People worldwide have always taken advantage of the plentiful seafood in bays, rivers and oceans. They have capitalized on ready and protein-rich food sources such as lobster and molluscs, harvesting them from shore by hand at low tide and in woven basket-like traps. They have also devised ways to preserve the glut from the summer catch for future use, such as smoking and drying.

European coastal dwellers have been eating lobster since the Stone Age. Despite meagre evidence of what they ate and how they cooked it, food historians suggest that most prehistoric coastal inhabitants regarded lobsters and many other shellfish as a valued secondary food. In *Food and Drink in Britain*, C. Anne Wilson notes an exception: for very poor backward British groups they were primary nourishment. Occasionally in areas such as the Scottish islands they were consumed during hard times, perhaps because gathering them was so labour-intensive, according to Jane Renfrew in *Food and Cooking in Prehistoric Britain*. Renfrew speculates that Scottish seaside folk during the Middle Stone Ages caught lobster on or near the shoreline using weighted baskets, the predecessors of modern lobster pots. It must have been simpler than using their deep-sea fishing boats. Inhabitants of or visitors to the Scottish island of Oronsay and Oban, a Scottish seaside town, probably ate them raw, boiled in water, smoked or roasted (in their shells) on hot stones.

Early inhabitants of the Italian peninsula were fans of the spiny lobster, as evidenced by the mosaic of a spiny lobster shell in ancient Pompeii. Rich Greeks and Romans enjoyed shellfish, sometimes paying steep prices for it. Romans from 54 BC to AD 407 considered all shellfish a treat, and even transported it inland over considerable distances.

Lobsters were so valuable to the ancient Peruvian culture, the Moche, that they appeared in the form of a lobster

The lobster effigy vessel is from the north coast of Peru and dates from around AD 50 to AD 800.

effigy vessel from the north coast of Peru around AD 50 to AD 800. The reddish-orange earthenware container was made from a mould, allowing mass production, then shaped with some hand modelling. There is no evidence of its owner or its purpose since the vessel is probably from looted burial sites. However, we know that lobster meat was used for food and that the shells made a light pink dye, ornaments and tools.

Lobster in Europe, AD 700 — the 1600s

Among northern Europeans, shellfish and fish consumption increased during the Viking period and afterwards for two reasons: better boats appropriate for deep-sea fishing were built, and there was pressure from both the Christian church and, especially in Britain, the desire to encourage shipbuilding and to train sailors. Fish, particularly fresh marine fish, became a status symbol and an important part of upper-class nourishment. Fish was much more available because much of northern Europe was just a day's journey by packhorse from the sea. Lobster consumption rose along with fish. But unlike fish, it needed to be cooked within two days of leaving salt water, making improved transportation crucial to its increased consumption. So it was available to those who could afford transportation.

Those who bought lobster could frequently afford the luxury of hiring someone to prepare it for them. These cooks shaped European cuisine, including how lobster was prepared. Two medieval books provide a glimpse into their world. In the early 1300s, the author of *Le Viandier de Taillevent* suggests eating lobster, also called saltwater crayfish, in vinegar after either boiling it in water and wine or cooking it in the oven. This cookery book is often mistakenly credited to Guillaume Tirel, alias Taillevent, (about 1310–1385), an influential chef in French royal households for whom the famous Parisian restaurant, among others, is named. But C. M. Woolgar debunks that myth in *Food: The History of Taste*, claiming that *Le Viandier* was already available before Tirel was born.

Le Ménagier de Paris, a 1393 guide for women's marriage conduct with household management instructions, was written by an elderly husband for his fifteen-year-old bride. Among other simple shellfish recipes, it gives directions for cooking *Homarus* and spiny lobsters. A lobster or crayfish soup required boiled, shelled and fried crustaceans served in a broth made from spices, including cinnamon, cloves and ginger, ground almonds and breadcrumbs moistened with water from cooked peas. The combination was boiled with a little vinegar. Vinegar was also the sauce for the spiny clawless lobster, which was either boiled or roasted (upside down); the clawed lobster was roasted in the oven with the added touch of spring onions (scallions).

Lobster found its way into prestigious households as a means of demonstrating affluence and political might, especially during feasts, which displayed a large array of species. In the early 1400s, for instance, the Bishop of Salisbury spread at least 42 different types of crustacea and fish on his table over a nine-month period. Many people living close to the shore sought out fish, oysters and especially shellfish (lobsters, crabs, shrimps and prawns). Boiling lobster was common in the mid-fifteenth century, but lobsters were now also eaten cold with vinegar. Meanwhile most of Britain's inland population wouldn't even recognize marine shellfish, having never seen them.

In 1548 an Act of the British Parliament converted Saturday into a fish day, requiring the population to eat seafood rather than meat. (To eat meat instead could be 'a serious offence'.) In the latter part of the sixteenth century, lobsters were probably among the fresh, pickled and salted fish that replaced the pricey meat eaten on 'fysshe days' by English coastal folk. Fish days were important in this century because they increased fish consumption, thereby conserving cattle, which were reserved for the navy. Fish days also spurred shipbuilding, expanding the ranks of mariners, and sparked the fishing business. The popularity of all shellfish in Europe continued to the late seventeenth century.

Fish days presented cooks with quite a challenge when faced with an elaborate banquet. Take the 1571 formal entrance of Elizabeth of Austria into Paris on her way to marry King Charles IX of France: twelve lobsters were on the diocese table, along with oysters, frogs, whale and much salted and fresh fish.

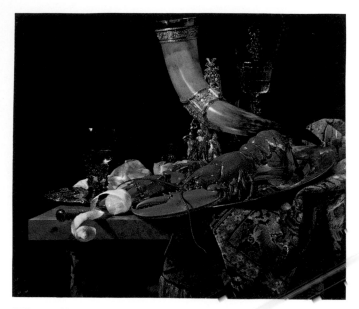

Willem Kalf, *Drinking Horn with a Lobster on a Table*, 1650s, oil on canvas. Lobsters were included in Dutch still lifes as symbols of luxury.

Hapsburg courts in Vienna and Prague revered lobster. Arcimboldo, the sixteenth-century Milanese painter, included a clawed lobster in his 1566 painting *Water*. The bold, red-orangey lobster rests prominently on the chest of the fantastical head-and-shoulder portrait composed entirely of sea creatures. This spectacular painting, by the court's portraitist (1562–1587), is part of the series *The Four Elements*, now in Vienna's Kunsthistorisches Museum. Although unappetizing, it is evidence of the lobster's familiarity to wealthy inlanders, and the esteem that it enjoyed among them.

Dutch painters also advertised the access to lobster enjoyed by the wealthy. Famous for his still lifes, Jan Davidsz. de Heem in the 1660s painted lifelike images of the iconic crustacean. The brilliant red lobster is prominent in both *Still*

Willem van Aelst, *Still-life with Fruit, Lobster and Silver Vessels*, 1660–70, oil on panel. Probably painted in Amsterdam, this Dutch still-life places a lobster centre stage, where it is as much a status symbol as the silver platter on which it rests.

Life with Fruit, Flowers, Glasses and Lobster and also *Still Life*, among the other trappings of the rich. A tray of smaller lobsters nestles next to a larger plate of fresh oysters in *The Allegory of Senses: Hearing, Touch and Taste* by Jan Brueghel and Hendrick van Balen – another example of lavish Renaissance feasts.

A Native American's Staple

Coastal Native Americans held shellfish and most seafood in high regard and relied on them as principal sources of protein and oil. For some tribes seafood was even the primary food for all occasions. The first hunters and gatherers from Maine and Narragansett Bay to Chesapeake Bay could not ignore more than eighty kinds of fish and shellfish that provided nourishment and were valuable enough to be traded. They caught them with gaffs, spears and dip nets in shallow water. Clam and oyster shell deposits that have been found on the east coast and eastern rivers testify to the huge amounts of shellfish consumed.

Lobsters were one common species the Native Americans enjoyed. In 1622, Englishman Thomas Morton's observation demonstrates the lobster's role in their feasts:

> This being knowne, they shall passe for a commodity to the inhabitants; for the Salvages [sic] will meete 500, or 1000 at a place where Lobsters come in with the tyde, to eate, and save dried for store; abiding in that place, feasting and sporting, a moneth or 6 weekes together.

Clambakes, which originated in New England with Native American tribes such as the Algonquins, often included

Shellfish are the main ingredient in this 2009 re-enactment of an American Indian clambake, at the Plimoth Plantation, a museum of the Wampanoag People and the Colonial English community in seventeenth-century Massachusetts.

lobsters. They dug a sandy pit on the beach near gathered lobsters and clams, lined it with stones and lit a fire over them. Covering the hot rocks with wet seaweed, they added lobster to the layers of clams and often corn.

The shellfish were cooked in a variety of ways: boiled, cooked on spits and 'rosted or dryed in the smoak', according to John Josselyn, a writer and skilled scientist who described his two New England visits to the British Royal Society in the 1670s in *John Josselyn, Colonial Traveler: A Critical Edition of Two Voyages to New England*. Maine lobsters were added to porridges, soups and stews. Other lobster species were also plentiful near the entrances to the Mississippi and Hudson rivers, the shores of the Gulf of Mexico and San Francisco Bay, and the Pacific Ocean.

Attitudes Towards American Lobster, 1600s

What was the equivalent of bread and butter to native peoples got a mixed reaction from the British arriving in the New World. Fish, including lobster, wasn't considered a substantial food, especially compared with the more desirable and nutritious meat. Seafood was boring to them and left them feeling unsatisfied. Allowing that fresh fish in British markets was often less than edible, it's no wonder that the notion of stinking fish probably evolved into the term 'fishy', or something that is suspect, according to Sandra L. Oliver, author of *Saltwater Foodways*. Puritans also brought along the lingering resentment and sense of deprivation from compulsory 'fysshe dayes' when there was insufficient meat, intensified by the lack of food in the early years of New England.

Yet in the cold Atlantic, settlers discovered the enormous *Homarus americanus*, with its whopping snapping claws, one slightly larger than the other, with strength enough to crush a live oyster. Perhaps some of the hundred or so Pilgrims who arrived off Cape Cod on the 180-ton vessel *Mayflower* in 1620 recognized it because they had eaten its counterpart, the slightly smaller European lobster, *H. gammarus*.

They had their first taste of the American lobster, along with other crustaceans, stumbled upon acorns and herbs and unearthed maize and beans in a Native American cache. To survive the first winter, the newcomers learned to eat what Native Americans provided from their stockpiles. It didn't take long for settlers to learn to catch their own shellfish, but other food was still scarce. In 1623, Governor William Bradford in Plymouth, Massachusetts, groused about being able to offer visitors only lobster, 'without bread or anything else but . . . water'. Sixty new settlers at the struggling Plymoth Plantation were also offered just lobster, fish and spring water.

'The least boy in the Plantation may both catch and eat what he will of them', wrote Reverend Francis Higginson of Salem in 1630. But even he was weary of them, even if 'they were so great, and fat, and luscious'. He reported they weighed from about 7 to over 11 kg (16–25 lb). Size wasn't always a virtue. Bypassing the nearly 6-foot lobsters, Adriaen van der Donck, the colonies' first lawyer, observed that 'those a foot long are better for serving at table'. Van der Donck, also the Dutch colonial governor, praised the bays, rivers and sea of New Netherland, brimming with lobster and 'fish of the finest qualities'.

Throughout New England these enormous shellfish were an easy supply of protein, but they were not valued. 'Their plenty makes them little esteemed and seldom eaten', wrote William Wood in *New England's Prospect*, 1634. Abundance bred contempt, so the colonists often only used lobster to fend off hunger and as cheap food for indentured servants and slaves. They fed it to pigs and used it as fertilizer and fish bait. There's one indignity that didn't befall the under-valued lobster: 'One of the most persistent and oft repeated food myths', wrote food historian Kathleen Curtin, is 'about laws being enacted to protect prisoners/servants from eating lobster more than three times a week – it never happened. [There is] not a shred of documentation.' Lobster got the same reaction from coastal folk as far north as Canada even in the eighteenth century, where people were embarrassed to eat the worthless creature and considered common oysters fit only for the poor. But eventually New Englanders began to appreciate lobster and fish for several reasons, according to the authors of *America's Founding Food*. They managed to overlook their reservations about local fish, particularly in light of their abundance and the possible financial gain from selling it. At the least, fresh seafood was an improvement over the ubiquitous dried fish necessary during times of scarcity.

Native Americans had enough influence on the immigrants' taste to inspire these verses by William Wood:

The luscious lobster with the crabfish raw,
The brinish oyster, mussel, periwig,
And tortoise sought for by the Indian squaw,
Which to the flats dance many a winter's jig,
To dive for cockles and to dig for clams.

Slowly European North Americans came around to appreciate this sometimes too abundant crustacean. Yet in Europe, lobsters, which had been consumed since the Stone Age on the coast, became a status symbol for the rich as they became less plentiful and more expensive to transport inland. As evidence of both their consumption and their value, they were taken as subjects by both artists and writers. But their consumption was limited until technological breakthroughs made them more easily available to the wider population.

2
From Main Course to Mass Market

Just throw a live one on the flames and *Voila!*, seared lobster. Perhaps that's how our distant relatives on the African coast discovered a way to roast the ubiquitous lobster when they first mastered fire some 1.9 million years ago.

While it was easy enough to cook, preserving lobster for future consumption took some ingenuity and a little longer to figure out. 'Dryed in the smoak' was how Native Americans conserved lobster for less bountiful days, according to seventeenth-century British author John Josselyn. In the 1600s the British invented a method that allowed them to keep the boiled meat for almost three months: the cooked lobsters were cloaked in brine-soaked rags and buried deep in sea-sand. (More commonly, they were boiled and eaten cold.)

Innovations Spur Popularity

The fishing industry had its ups and downs, depending on the availability of fish and whether the government imposed fish days, which were abolished during the late 1500s. Even when fresh fish was costly and rare, the wealthy British purchased it. But the poor were thoroughly tired of eating salted fish and mediocre freshwater fish. They wanted more seafood choices and that inspired the fishing enterprises to find ways to bring fresh white fish, including lobster, to market more affordably.

Innovations also increased the demand for lobster. One of the first came as early as the 1500s. The Dutch built tanks or wells in the holds of sailing ships, which, according to author C. Anne Wilson, 'ran from wall to wall across the ship, and its sides were perforated so that the seawater could circulate among the fish put to swim inside', something like a swimming pool on a cruise ship. By the 1600s, the English had adopted the Dutch technique and built a fleet of well-vessels, or 'smacks', that kept expensive seafood alive during long journeys back to London. This method worked well for lobster too. Another strategy was to hold lobsters and turbot in rock pools or tidal ponds, such as those caught close to

The *Whistler*, a smack boat built in 1868 and lying on its side in the Noank, Connecticut harbour, probably carried fresh lobster and seafood in the seawater tank built into the hold of the vessel.

Tynemouth on the northern English coast (similar to lobster pounds today), and deliver them alive to London in well-vessels. It would be over a hundred years before well-vessels reached the New World.

Perishability prevented lobster from becoming a commonly eaten seafood. But the British continued to experiment with different preservation techniques. Potted lobster, in vogue with the wealthy during the seventeenth century, was served with the lighter second course. Cooked lobster meat was covered in butter in a stoneware pot and kept cold. As with cold fish pies sealed in butter, such dishes could last up to a year, making it possible to carry preserved lobster and other seafood further inland. Potted lobster was savoured throughout the 1700s, and recipes for it eventually appeared in America.

Across the Channel in France, lobster consumption got a boost from the evolution of cooking. In his review of Barbara Ketcham Wheaton's book *Savoring the Past*, Professor Ronald W. Tobin attributed it to 'the flowering of cookery between 1650 and 1789 [that was] . . . a result of an abundance of ingredients, a desire for professional advancement on the part of cooks, and a need for conspicuous display of wealth by the privileged classes, the better to maintain their status.' And these crustaceans helped chefs satisfy the varied palates of wealthy Christian households during meatless days.

Chefs might have used lobster recipes from the 1651 version of *Le Cuisinier françois* [*sic*] or *The French Cook* by François Pierre de la Varenne, whose reputation and wildly popular cookbook (30 editions in 75 years) influenced many European kitchens. La Varenne, as he is often known, recommended simply boiling the shellfish in a seasoned bouillon and serving it with vinegar and parsley. A fancier version suggested fricasséed lobster pieces with a white sauce made with butter, parsley, a bit of verjuice (unripe grape juice used like lemon juice is today) combined with egg yolks and a dash of nutmeg. The lobster 'feet' were for garnish.

If La Varenne gets credit for 'the first great French cookbook' then Vincent la Chapelle's *The Modern Cook* (1733) has the honour of being the landmark for the diffusion of France's culinary expertise, according to Wheaton. In his 1744 edition La Chapelle offered several ways to prepare lobster after boiling it in salted water. There was nothing new about serving the boiled shellfish cold with parsley. But he described an Italian version that may be one of the first examples of the French adding meat gravy, a meat reduction sauce and even truffles. Sliced lobster meat was added to a 'stew-pan' with butter, onion, parsley, mushrooms and truffles, all mois- tened with gravy and champagne. Then it was seasoned with pepper, salt, sweet herbs and a leek like bulb that had a gentle garlic flavour, and stewed. Once it was thickened with 'cullis' (a veal and lamb broth reduction) and a final touch of oil and lemon juice, the lobster was ready to be delivered as what La Chapelle called a hot 'dainty' dish. He favoured a cullis made from the crushed lobster shells for his lobster ragout.

While the affluent French had lobster ragout and the posh British devoured rich potted lobster, their adventurous New World compatriots made many a meal of plain boiled lobster without sauce or seasoning. Living hand to mouth, the Pilgrims weren't excited about lobster (or any seafood) and yearned for the food that arrived on infrequent ships from England. But by the mid-1700s they had discovered how to pickle lobsters. 'Lobsters are likewise plentifully caught hereabouts, pickled much in the same way as oysters, and sent to several places', wrote Swedish naturalist Peter Kalm in his 1750 New World travelogue. Kalm had seen live lobsters in the bustling New York market.

For trailblazers who sailed east, shellfish preservation wasn't foremost in their minds. But they were observant. In the late 1700s explorers such as Captain Tobias Furneaux observed marine crayfish (spiny lobster) in parts of Australia. In 1773 Furneaux found proof that they were sustenance for Tasmanian Aborigines. 'In the middle [of the "native's" huts] is the fire-place, surrounded with heaps of muscle, pearly scallop, and cray-fish shells; which I believe to be their chief food, though we could not find any of them,' he wrote. Closer to the turn of the century, another adventurer, J.J.H. Labillardière, described how the locals caught them in another Tasmanian bay: 'The women took each a basket, and were followed by their daughters, who did the same. Getting on the rocks that projected into the sea, they plunged them to the bottom in search of shellfish.'

No matter where in the world lobsters were found, every-one who cooked them was worried about their freshness. Both British and American cooks were advised about purchas-ing this delicate, fast-spoiling crustacean because it must be cooked alive and was dangerous to eat if it wasn't. Late sev-enteenth- and eighteenth-century British cookbooks revealed schemes by unreliable purveyors at fish markets, including telltale plugs in the claws that held in extra water to add weight. On the other side of the Atlantic, cooks got advice about quality. In 1796 Amelia Simmons advised how to choose the market's freshest lobster and fish in *American Cookery*:

> Every species . . . are best fresh from the water . . . [and] may be transported by land many miles, find a good mar-ket, and retain a good relish; but as generally, live ones are bought first, deceits are used to give them a freshness of appearance . . . your smell must approve or denounce them, and be your safest guide.

Even when fresh, lobster required some dressing up to be palatable. Disguising seafood with sauce made it more appealing and was common in both England and the colonies. Lobster was often one of many ingredients in sauces; rarely was it the main course. British cookery writer Hannah Glasse included recipes for both sauces and main courses in her 1747 edition of *The Art of Cookery Made Plain and Easy*. According to Kate Colquhoun in *Taste*, Glasse suggested lobsters be 'boiled and split or roasted (for far too long, by our standards)'. The cooked lobster then joined other baked and fried fish drenched in Glasse's sauces that were seafood combinations including more lobster, and then adorned with cockles, butter, lemon, oysters or wine. A widow supporting a flock of children, Glasse was one of two British women who commanded the unpretentious, middle-class cookbook market, regularly delivering new editions. Colquhoun said that Glasse knew her audience 'could not afford French cooks or cooking' but relished entertaining, so she targeted 'ordinary, if financially comfortable townswomen . . . who wanted to slough off the burden of teaching their staff how to cook'. Her uncommon recipe for lobster as the main course, though she didn't know it, was perhaps one of the predecessors of the haute cuisine preparations on the horizon. However, Glasse (even posthumously) bears no responsibility for the imminent thunderous popularity of *Homarus americanus*. Technology, not taste, gets most of the credit.

Lobsters Travel to Market

As in Europe, sailing well-vessels played a pivotal role in the North American commercial exploitation of lobsters, especially as the population exploded in New York City and erupted up the New England coast. In the mid-1700s, anyone near an urban market could buy a live three-pound (1.4 kg) lobster for about three cents, including in New York, which had nearby lobster smacks that were first operated in Long Island Sound. It is easy to imagine that one of the many Dutchmen who settled in the area instigated the development of these vessels, which had been in use in Holland since the 1500s.

By 1800 New York fishermen couldn't keep up with the demand. 'Smackmen', who could store thousands of lobsters for several days or more, were delivering these crustaceans to New York and Boston markets in the early 1820s from southern Maine, and by the 1840s from the central Maine coast.

George Dempster, one of the first fishmongers to transport fish to affluent London customers, used ice instead. In about 1820 he managed this expensive feat by means of new

Edward William Cooke, *Lobster Pots, Ventnor*, 1835. The well-vessels might have picked up lobsters from fishermen using these lobster baskets made on Britain's Isle of Wight.

ice-making machinery that replaced the natural Norwegian and Icelandic ice the new steam trawlers had been using. The trawlers cut the time it took to deliver catches to English fishing ports from the North Sea's rich banks. Premium Scotch salmon delivered in pristine condition, not lobster, fetched the best price. Cheaper ice and improved railways soon made it feasible to bring bright-eyed fish and lively shellfish to inland markets, especially for those willing to pay for it.

What was the effect of the new ice-making capability and speedy trawlers on lobster? The ice made it possible to sell Norway lobsters in Europe. Year round, their small claws were bound with cord and gently packed in heather dampened by seawater; in the summer, they travelled on a bed of ice as well.

From the Plate to the Tin

Experimentation in the kitchen was driven less by technology than by culinary imagination. In the early 1800s British cookery writers continued to target the middle classes, much like in the previous century, providing lobster sauce recipes. Lobster was low on the food chain for the bourgeoisie – even lower than fish that was a clear second to butcher's meat. While dinner-party suggestions included the ever-favourite cod's head and Dutch turbot, chopped lobster flesh was relegated to sauce made with melted butter, embellished with fish stock, lemon juice and oysters. Catherine Dickens, Charles Dickens's wife, accompanied fish with lobster sauce in one of her menus for a grand dinner in 1852. Her cookbook *What Shall We Have for Dinner?*, written under the pseudonym Lady Maria Clutterbuck, included all-occasion menus and some recipes for hostesses fretting about impressing their guests. Her menus mirrored solidly upper-middle-class life in London and indicated that lobster's status might be on the rise through a few exceptions such as lobster with shrimp sauce and lobster curry.

Lobsters were anything but exotic in coastal America. New Englanders had to feed their families the ubiquitous lobster, and as any inventive cook will do, they found new ways to prepare it and adapted many of the British recipes. Many recipes directed that it 'be added to sauces, scalloped, fricasséed, stewed, devilled, used in soup or bisque, made into croquettes, in *vol au vents*, and very, very often in salad', wrote Oliver. In other words, in most cases, rendered unrecognizable.

Stewing and fricasséeing lobster were common preparation methods for eighteenth- and nineteenth-century New England cooks. Both techniques involved simmering bits of lobster in cream or white wine with a dash of cayenne, salt, pepper, nutmeg and powdered nutmeg shell (mace). They even stewed lobster patties. Clearly the now-exalted lobster held

'Menu du restaurant Maxim's en 1896', Paris, rue Royale. Lobster was on the menu in both England and France in the 1800s.

44

no special place in eighteenth- and nineteenth-century American diets. By the early 1800s buying boiled lobster was a common timesaving step for cooks. They could clean it and add it to sauces and salads, since consumers liked lobster best in a prepared dish. If housewives bought a live lobster that showed no signs of damage and had all its appendages, they still had to cook it within two days. Little did they know of the modern convenience that would shortly be on their doorstep.

A batch of European breakthroughs at the turn of the nineteenth century influenced both the quality and the availability of North Atlantic lobster, which formerly was affordable beyond the coast only for the wealthy. Warring Britain and France were losing more soldiers and sailors to disease caused by pitiful nutrition than to combat. Deadly rations for their warriors prompted the French government to sponsor a 1795 contest that offered 12,000 francs to the creator of the best-preserved food. French chef Nicolas Appert revealed his discovery of a method for bottling food in 1803 and won the prize seven years later. For the French navy he prepared tasty stews, meats, vegetables and drinks that were packed into glass bottles, closed with cork stoppers, sealed with waxy pitch and finally heated to prevent spoiling. Several years later the British Royal Navy was enjoying similar food, but in iron canisters sealed with tin. In 1810 the British patent for the tin can, a tin-plated steel container, was awarded to Peter Durand. Almost a decade later, well after Appert's methods were printed in *The Art of Preserving*, a London cannery named Donkin-Hall was primed to produce tinned food. The stage was set for the future canning of lobster.

In Australia Nathan Ogle touted the fishing prospects, a pitch to the English to join the colony: 'The fish are without number, from the whale to the shrimp . . . Cockles, muscles, oysters, cray-fish, prawns, teem all along the coasts.' In his

This fisherman carried a lobster basket conveniently on his head, a style used in Brittany, France for many years.

of canned goods, resulting in cheaper products and introducing food that had been preserved in cans to millions of Americans. By the time soldiers saw this canned meal, they could, if they were lucky, use the can opener that was invented in 1858, but probably most employed bayonets, pocket-knives, rifles, rocks or the hammer and chisel.

It took a wave of permanent migration, rather than tourists (and a war or two) to spark the demand for rock lobster in Australia. But it began with a few individuals. Around 1848 Edward Back found the crustaceans teeming in the waters and coral reefs around Rottnest Island near Fremantle, where he was employed as a marine pilot. Crayfish loved the shipwrecks and the hazardous reefs that caused them. Most likely what he saw was the species common to Western Australia's waters, the western rock lobster or *Panulirus cygnus*, frequently called crayfish, spiny lobster, crawfish and *langouste*.

Beginning in 1850, the first convicts from England – ten thousand of them – landed over a period of eighteen years in Swan River Colony on the Swan River that runs through Fremantle to the sea, providing the labour needed to build the fishing industry such as 'fishers, fishmongers, shipwrights and sailmakers', wrote Howard Gray in *The Western Rock Lobster: Panulirus cygnus*. That influx of Europeans, especially in the late 1800s, ignited the creation of the world's largest rock lobster fishery in Australia, much as the Europeans' knowhow had influenced lobster fishing in North America. They continued to use the hoop nets and later added pots and baited traps of various designs and materials. Just as it took time and resources to establish the western rock lobster fisheries, it required persistence and awareness to ignite the spiny lobster canning business. Australians had been canning fish since 1878, but did not dabble in canning lobster until the early 1900s. Clearly there was a market because in the meantime South Africa's production, which had begun in the 1870s, flourished, especially during World War I.

With the advent of World War II, US troops stationed at Fremantle and Perth liked the local shellfish. 'Rock lobsters were eagerly sought by the United States service personnel . . . a luxury food,' wrote Gray. Between 1943 and 1945, he added, 'approximately 3 million cans of rock lobster had been supplied to the Defense Forces, reaching members of the services in England, Malaya, Singapore and Ceylon, as well

49

3
Lobster Takes Centre Stage

Lobster had its extended coming-out party in North America from the mid-1800s to the mid-1900s. Not only was the crustacean now recognizable to the hordes of leisure-class Maine vacationers who could afford fresh lobster, but they now demanded it back home in their urban restaurants. The recipes in that period are just a reflection of the significant shift in attitudes towards lobster. Those acquainted with the debutante shunned the old-fashioned dishes of lobster forcemeat and potted lobster. Other variations such as stewed lobster were still prepared but were renamed. Where sauce was once used to disguise lobster, it now dressed up the distinguishable meat into dreamy, prestigious dishes. 'Now boiled or baked, served in a Newburg [sic] sauce (the updated version of fricassée), or in a salad or chowder, lobster had assumed its modern forms', said Keith Stavely and Kathleen Fitzgerald, describing lobster's coming-out attire.

Lobster Salad and Clambakes

Lobster in various configurations has become a feature of the good life in many parts of the world. Lobster salad, for example, has been popular in America since the 1800s, and today there are countless ways to prepare it. A recipe appeared as early as 1833 in Lydia Maria Child's *The American Frugal Housewife* that contained lettuce and the meat of one lobster dressed with cayenne, egg yolks, mustard, oil, vinegar and salt. Lobsters were fetched from the market, so Child also gave instructions for appraising freshness: a good sign is if while holding 'the end of a lobster' it 'springs back hard and firm'; on the other hand, 'if they move flabbily, it is not a good omen'. Lobster salad was probably an improvement on the fifteenth-century British version served with vinegar.

As early as 1851, lobster salad was on the menu at the Revere House in Boston, which catered to both European royalty and American presidents. This tasty salad was offered at President Andrew Johnson's parties and President William H. Taft's honorary dinner in Vermont as well as to the Russian fleet visiting Boston. With the invention of the lobster roll,

Lobster rolls, a popular, portable treat, are typically made from lobster salad stuffed into a hot dog bun.

By the late 1800s, trains and boats brought tourists to the Rhode Island shore where commercial clambakes were wildly popular. At Rocky Point, Rhode Island, crowds of close to ten thousand people could be fed. Clambake popularity mushroomed after the Civil War and eventually they merged with picnics, becoming useful at fundraisers and political rallies. They were also the forerunners of today's ubiquitous food festivals. Today, lobsters accompanying clambakes have become standard fare along the entire coast but are no longer exclusive to New England.

Fish chowders, often part of clambakes even today, became a leisure food rather than subsistence grub in America by the middle of the eighteenth century. Shellfish such as lobster appear almost as frequently as fish in chowder recipes of the early 1900s. Originally survival fare in many countries, the stew that emerged from Brittany in the 1500s and 1600s was spread by European fishing fleets to north-eastern Canada and to the New England coast. The English word 'chowder'

A lobster bake in Islesboro, Maine, 1993.

probably derives from *chaudière* – cauldron – and from the name for a fisherman's stew, *la chaudrée*.

The Cinderella-like transformation from subsistence rations to haute cuisine took a couple of centuries longer in America than in Europe. The Europeans did have a head start, since North America and Australia were settled later. Availability had a lot to do with it. An early tourist, Hildegard Hawthorne, travelling with her sister, witnessed the delivery of mounds of lobsters in 1916 in Portland, Maine. They were scooped out of the fishing smacks, claws pegged, and packed into barrels for their journey to New York. It was enough to whet her appetite: 'but let's go and eat . . . a nice broiled lobster, now . . . They lose their spirit by the time they reach N'York. This is the place for 'em', she wrote.

New Yorkers and others, unworried about their lost spirit, now favoured the fresh lobsters that better transportation provided, and they had the money to pay for them. America finally had an upper class filled with the super-rich, who made their money in a huge post-Civil War industrial expansion, many of whom were self-indulgent and extravagant. And cookbooks had the lavish recipes they desired. Fannie Farmer declared in her 1896 *Boston Cooking-School Cook Book* that 'Lobsters belong to the highest order of Crustaceans', and offered some of the most popular preparations including the simplified Lobster à la Newberg and Lobster à la Delmonico.

One version of the creation of Lobster à la Newberg, a still-coveted creamy casserole, was perhaps made famous in 1876 at Delmonico's, a 'true palace of haute cuisine' in New York's Madison Square. Charles Delmonico, apparently introduced to the seafood preparation by sea captain and fruit importer Ben Wenberg, who had just returned from a Cuban cruise, was taken with the dish and named it 'Lobster à la

Davidson, author of *Mediterranean Seafood*, scoffed at the idea that either *américaine* or *armoricaine* is correct, though he believed the ingredients certainly suggested a Mediterranean origin. He offered instead an 'indisputably' Provençal spiny lobster recipe where the cooked meat is dipped in a sauce made of a shallot, anchovies, French mustard, parsley, garlic, lemon juice and olive oil. Both the Greeks and Turks serve cold lobster with a dressing of lemon juice, olive oil and parsley, according to Davidson.

Spiny lobsters found in the Indo-Pacific waters are considered by many to taste as good as *Homarus* lobsters. They

An unusual 1900s version of *Homard à l'Armoricaine*, also known as Lobster *à l'Américaine*.

have a huge following, especially if cookbooks are any indication. Davidson also wrote a thorough handbook about the *Seafood of South-East Asia* that includes some of the many Asian spiny lobsters and recipes. While he wrote that the *Panulirus ornatus* or 'brocade-beautiful lobster' (*jin xiu long xia* in Chinese), often found in Vietnam, is not the most desirable to devour, Davidson suggested recipes for others such as the mud spiny lobster (*P. polyphagus*). He thought this was an excellent species and invented a recipe for cooked lobster dressed with homemade mayonnaise, a bit of durian (a Malaysian fruit) and fresh pineapple cubes, served chilled in the pineapple shell with a tiny amount of black pepper. Davidson also suggested that the slipper lobster meat, though not 'quite up to the standard of good . . . spiny lobsters', was certainly 'worth eating', using typical recipes for crabs and prawns.

Clawed and clawless lobsters are frequently used interchangeably in recipes, such as in the Lobster *à la Parisienne* recipe in *Larousse Gastronomique*. Recipes abound for this delicious crustacean. There are two noteworthy formulas for *langouste* or spiny lobsters from *Larousse* – a Spanish version with unsweetened chocolate in a tomato sauce flavoured with almonds, cinnamon chocolate, hazelnuts and red sweet peppers, and a Chinese recipe where it is browned in sesame oil with chives, onions and fresh ginger. But the southern Chinese have long been connoisseurs of lobster. In Guangzhou, the capital of Guangdong province and perhaps China's culinary mecca, their famous delicate lobster Cantonese dish combines the shellfish and its sauce with marinated ground pork, minced seasonings and lightly beaten egg. Lobster soup is a favourite in many countries, including South Africa where boiled rock lobster tails are added to a broth of butter, cream, garlic, lemon rind, nutmeg, onions, tomatoes and white wine.

Sir John Tenniel, 'Lobster'. This wood engraving is for Lewis Carroll's book *Alice's Adventures in Wonderland* (1865).

Whether cooked or displayed in a museum, lobster's popularity has transformed it into an icon. The crustacean was mentioned in the well-known children's tale *Alice's Adventures in Wonderland* (1865) and its trap is hanging in Alexander Calder's mobile *Lobster Trap and Fish Tail* (1939) in New York's Museum of Modern Art. Giant mutant lobsters figure in the surreal nightmare of the 1970 Japanese film *Space Amoeba*.

Lobster Festivals

While native people worldwide had gatherings that left middens, contemporary folk have turned to a different mode of celebrating the marine shellfish that creates a lot of refuse but may not leave any fossils. Lobster festivals are held all over the world including in Africa, America, Australia and Canada. Luederitz, a seaside town in Namibia, held their first rock lobster festival in 2008.

The annual Shediac Lobster Festival, begun in 1949, is celebrated in Shediac, New Brunswick, Canada, which calls itself 'The Lobster Capital of the World', and is the home of reputedly the world's largest lobster sculpture. The Maine celebration of their icon, the American lobster, is a five-day event held on Rockland's waterfront, a mid-coast fishing town that author and essayist David Foster Wallace called '*the nerve stem of* Maine's lobster industry'. It attracted about 60,000 attendees in 2008. Almost 8,618 kg (19,000 lb) of lobsters were boiled in the 'World's Largest Lobster Cooker' and eaten simply – alongside a tiny cup filled with butter and an ear of corn, with a set of metal crackers and a plastic pick, a lobster bib and disposable towelettes. Lobster is also transformed

This 90-ton 'Giant Lobster' sculpture is in Shediac, New Brunswick, Canada, which has had an annual lobster festival since 1949.

A plastic bib is part of the standard equipment that comes with a North American boiled lobster.

into bisque, dumplings, salads, ravioli, rolls and turnovers. Despite the success of both the festivals, there is a danger to the North American lobster industry that is right out in the open.

Lobster Impostors

You can buy knock-off lobster, like knock-off designer hand-bags and watches, and you don't have to go to your local street vendor to find it. Until recently you could find it at Rubio's Fresh Mexican Grill, a US restaurant chain based in California. Rubio's used langostino rather than real lobster for its 'lobster burrito' and 'lobster taco'.

'No matter what you call it, "squat" isn't lobster', said one headline. Langostino is not lobster at all, even though it is sometimes called squat lobster, or even tuna or pelagic red crab. Nor is it a prawn or shrimp. Langostino is a cousin of hermit and porcelain crabs, distant kin of true crabs. (Although langostino is Spanish for prawn, it is used to describe a variety of shellfish species in the Galatheidae family.) So how can US restaurants get away with calling langostino 'lobster'? Only four varieties of squat lobster have legal approval by the US Food and Drug Administration (FDA) to use the moniker 'langostino lobster', even though they are not authentic lobster. While this only reinforces the confusion in America, there's more to bewilder knowledgeable diners worldwide. Just look at this tangle of names and definitions: langostino is easily mistaken for langoustine, a true or clawed lobster (*Nephrops norvegicus*, also with many nicknames). Nor are they spiny lob-sters, also called *langouste* in France. In some Caribbean islands and in Cuba, *langostino* means freshwater crayfish. Some of the most commercially important squat lobsters, out of the more than nine hundred species worldwide, are from Chile, El Salvador and New Zealand (especially the Eastern Pacific) and off the European coast.

Although Rubio's renamed their dish 'langostino lobster burrito' after an out-of-court settlement, and seem to have quit serving it, some seafood chains have continued the use of langostino to represent true lobster on menus. For instance, the 'buttered lobster bites' offered periodically at Long John Silver's fast-food restaurants include breaded langostino lobster with a host of food additives that enhance flavouring, texture or thickening.

Restaurant chains are not the only businesses to take advantage of the confusion and use the cachet of the word 'lobster' to sell a fake. Now that the FDA no longer requires US companies to label their seafood products 'imitation', the agency has further diluted the definition of genuine lobster, allowing instead 'lobster-flavoured seafood'. In America, Lobster Delights, made by Seattle-based Trident Seafoods Corporation (under its Louis Kemp brand), offers the 'mild flavour of lobster in firm, moist chunks', according to its website description. 'Mild' is an understatement, given that the product, primarily made of wild Alaskan pollock, contains '2 per cent or less of . . . lobster meat' and 'artificial lobster flavour'. They intentionally offer this as an affordable

Will F. Phillips, 'Who's a lobster?', 1899.

alternative to the real thing. *Surimi* (or formed fish) has been made for centuries by the Japanese, who consider it a legitimate food item. A concoction of minced white fish such as Alaskan pollock, created to look and taste like lobster chunks and other seafood (crab legs, scallops and shrimp), *surimi* is considered a seafood imitation in North America, where manufacturers copy the look of the shellfish by painting it a shade of orange. Not everyone recognizes *surimi* when they eat it but it is not uncommon to find this faux seafood in North American markets and in low-priced dining establishments in casseroles, salads and soups. Perhaps imitation is the sincerest form of flattery.

So lobster's coming out is over and it's been so successful that there are knock-offs. With its seemingly endless popularity and availability, we've created an array of dishes in which to enjoy it and even savour arguing over the origin of some of the more extravagant recipes. We won't be able to resolve whether it was a Parisian chef or a nameless cook in Brittany who created Lobster *à l'Américaine*. But that pales in comparison to the current feuds that threaten the party.

4
Lobster Controversies

'Is the lobster a fish?' That question was at the core of the British–French spat over Newfoundland fishing rights, or that was how it appeared at first. The quarrel began in the late 1800s when predictions of the impending extinction of the coveted crustacean reached fever pitch in the vigorous lobster canning industry on the north-eastern coast of North America.

If lobsters were considered fish, then they were covered by terms of treaties between Britain and France giving the French the right to fish, otherwise the fishing industry's operations were illegal. But here is a single instance of many territorial clashes that never got decided; this one was stymied by various claims by Newfoundland and France that prevented an international arbitration panel from coming to a conclusion. One thing was clear though: the consensus around 1902 among zoologists at the time was that the lobster was not classified as a fish; it was a marine animal.

According to one version in the *New York Times* in 1902, French naturalist and zoologist Georges Cuvier (1769–1832) captured the essence of the conflict: 'What is a lobster?' he once asked a student.

'A red fish that walks backward', was the reply.

'You are quite right,' commented Cuvier, 'except in three small particulars. It is not a fish, it is not red, and it does not walk backward.'

Disputes abound in the lobstering world: about fishing territories; about whether a lobster is a fish; if these ancient crustaceans feel pain or not; or how to treat them humanely. Private rows or transgressions between individual lobster trappers are taken for granted, especially given the secrecy with which they guard their individual fishing grounds. But as the lobster and fishing industries have changed, so have the disputes. They involve nations in full view of the public.

The Lobster War

Known as the 'Lobster War', a conflict surfaced between France and Brazil in 1963 over fishing grounds off the latter's coast that again hinged on whether lobsters were fish. The two nations were fighting over the plentiful shellfish on Brazil's section of the continental shelf, an area that all countries have the rights to, whether the natural resources are under or on the shelves, according to the 1958 Geneva Convention. However, the convention never explicitly included 'crustacea or swimming species'. Economically both the French Bretons and the northern Brazilians needed the lobsters.

So the French argued that lobsters were similar to fish that *swim around* rather than rest on or under the shelf. The Brazilians claimed that the shellfish were *crawlers* and were on the shelf. Earlier skirmishes had escalated into a crisis in January when Brazilian authorities seized several French vessels and ordered the Breton lobstermen to stop fishing and retreat beyond 100 km (62 miles) from the shore. The French sent their warship *Tartu* to defend them amid rumoured

The ubiquitous spiny lobsters are found primarily in warm waters, but can adapt to many environments. This one, *Palinurus elephas*, is found in parts of the Mediterranean and south-west Europe.

sightings of the Brazilian navy. The lobster trawlers, outfitted with special tanks, returned to Brest, France but the dispute continued. Both sides withdrew visiting delegations and ambassadors. Eventually, they returned their ambassadors and restarted the exchanges but without directly settling the disagreement.

Disagreements probably will continue as lobstermen worldwide jockey for the richest grounds. Depleted lobster stock, more sophisticated equipment for storage and better navigation devices have set the stage for more intense international competition and conflict.

Japanese chefs have invented many different ways of preparing lobster.

Cultural Differences

Just as there are disputes over lobster fishing territory, there are disagreements over how to treat the individual lobster. What is considered an accepted practice in one society, such as serving live lobster sashimi or boiling lobsters alive, is considered torture in another. Whether lobsters feel pain is an issue that has heated up in recent years and, in some cases, has boiled over.

A video on YouTube shows a Japanese chef preparing live lobster sashimi. Preparing live seafood is an honour for this chef, who cuts it so skilfully that it doesn't die before it arrives at the table, so that the esteemed guest eats an exceptionally fresh and expertly prepared dish. 'There is no danger in eating raw or undercooked lobster, as the splendour of thinly sliced lobster sashimi will testify', opined chef Rick Stein in his seafood cookbook. To some Westerners or animal rights proponents, it looks savage to see a chef ripping

Boiling lobsters in a tall aluminium pan is a global practice and is best done with salted water.

the body from a squirming clawed lobster tail, and then quickly slicing the meat out of the flapping tail, gently laying the motionless eviscerated shell on its back on a plate. The chef delicately plants the entire remaining writhing body belly-down on a mound of emerald-green seaweed, next to the now-still tail shell filled with its own live meat.

Submerging live lobsters in a tall silver pan of boiling water may be the ultimate in cruelty, and yet it is a long-standing tradition worldwide. That the lobster may drown first if the cook doesn't use salted water, since it cannot survive in fresh, or may take longer than a few seconds to die, is unimportant to some and beastly to others. The discomfort and difficulty people have with cooking live lobsters is also reflective of an issue we are uncomfortable with – killing our own food. As writer Trevor Corson says, 'We want our food to have been happy in death.' Or at least comfortable in the process

Do Lobsters Feel Pain?

'Flannel jackets to preserve them from the chill' was what some 'some tender-hearted American females' wanted for live lobsters on sale that were 'exposed on ice' in a Newfoundland, Canada market. Their demands gave them 'fleeting newspaper notoriety' wrote an anonymous author of a 1902 *New York Times* article, who reported that there was the occasional 'outcry over this cruelty' of boiling lobsters alive, which was not 'so familiar a fact' then.

A more serious report surfaced in a 1930 Berlin court case when a German colonel objected to a fish merchant who laid out a lobster in his store window with its claws lashed together with twine. Colonel Haroun al Rashid Bey, a decorated war pilot 'who became a Turk when adopted by a Turkish family', was outraged at the lobster's treatment and considered it torture. 'I am the possessor of the highest German medal for life saving', he explained. 'But it is of equal concern to me whether I come to the rescue of a human being or an animal who is suffering.' The fishmonger faced several experts, including the director of the Berlin aquarium and a biology professor, in the court proceedings. Not unexpectedly, the professor 'testified that it was difficult to state whether a lobster had any feelings, or suffered, since only the lobster itself could tell'. The aquarium director asserted 'that the lobster had feelings' and that the merchant's treatment was cruel. Surprisingly the court agreed with the director and the colonel. The merchant was fined the equivalent of £6 ($10), which was suspended because he couldn't have known that he was torturing the lobster.

A colourful spiny lobster underwater flaunts its 10 legs, demonstrating its membership in the decapod family and in the larger family of insects, scorpions and spiders.

In a 1930s pamphlet The Massachusetts Society for the Prevention of Cruelty to Animals reported frequent complaints about lobster handling but explained that the courts refused to pursue the cases because 'the lobster was of too low a form of life in its nervous structure to suffer pain as we know it'.

That's still the question at the centre of the battle today – is the lobster's nervous system complex enough to feel pain? American author David Foster Wallace called lobsters 'giant sea insects', noting that they are in the larger family (or phylum) that includes 'insects, spiders, crustaceans and centipedes/millipedes'. So we're worried about killing an insect? Canada's Clearwater Seafoods Limited Partnership's website says that lobsters have a 'very primitive nervous system similar to that of a grasshopper', enabling them to respond to 'very basic stimuli contained within their habitat'. Clearwater maintains that lobsters die almost instantly after plunging into boiling water, and contends that scientific research proves the tail twitching, which lasts for about a minute, is simply 'an involuntary muscle contraction'. The lobster insect analogy is also supported by Dr Robert Bayer, animal and veterinary sciences professor and executive director of the Lobster Institute at the University of Maine. 'Lobsters have no brain,' said Bayer, 'they don't have the psychological software to process pain.' They experience temperature variation and respond to other changes in their environment. But they're also somewhat lacking in nerve cells – with only about 100,000 neurons (a human has roughly 1 billion neurons). Peppered with questions about whether boiling lobsters is humane, the institute assigned researchers to study the shellfish's nervous systems, and they agreed with Clearwater – only organisms with more complex nervous systems experience pain.

A hotel for lobsters? The Clearwater Seafoods Limited Partnership has developed a unique storage system for lobsters.

Scientists on the other side of the argument claim that lobsters have more elaborate nervous systems that permit them to experience distress. They cite a 2009 study that investigated how another crustacean, the hermit crab, would react to tiny electric shocks to its abdomen from wires attached to the shell. It was conducted by Professor Bob Elwood, animal behaviour professor at Queen's University in Belfast, Ireland, and published in the *British Journal of Animal Behaviour*. As in his 2007 study on prawns, he and his colleagues found that the crab noticed the shocks and left its shell for a new one. Elwood doesn't think this behaviour is a simple reflex but believes that these behaviours are similar to observed pain reactions in mammals. 'With vertebrates we are asked to err on the side of caution and I believe this is the approach to take with these crustaceans.' While the clashes continue about whether lobsters feel pain and distress when they move from the ocean to our tables, Clearwater Seafoods has a different concern.

Losing weight is one thing Clearwater Seafoods does not want its lobsters to do while on their way to a customer. To be on the safe side, Clearwater, concerned about the quality of the lobsters they ship around the world, built a lobster

Lobsters hibernate in individual lobster drawers in one of three dry-land pound storage facilities in Nova Scotia, Canada. These healthy shellfish may live up to six months.

recovery facility near the Louisville, Kentucky airport so the crustaceans could recuperate before continuing with their journey. If they can experience stress, why not distress?

Global Sympathy Grows

Whole Foods Market, the American natural-foods retailer, was concerned about humane treatment of live lobsters on their voyage to customers and in 2005 established a team to evaluate each step of the supply chain. Working with Clearwater Seafoods, they invented single lobster condos, using stacked pvc pipes as private homes for in-store tanks, and specially designed holding compartments for individual crustaceans during storage that can last for months. But a year later Whole Foods, with more than 260 stores in the us and five in the uk, stopped carrying live lobster because nothing satisfied their concern for the humane treatment of the shellfish (and perhaps to appease animal rights groups). So did Safeway, the first large traditional grocer with about 1,700 Canadian and us stores, who bailed out because of declining sales. Given the trend in large retailers towards discontinuing carrying live lobster, it is becoming harder to find live lobsters to cook at home. All is not lost though: Whole Foods continues to offer packaged frozen raw lobster tails and cooked meat.

According to a 2005 survey by the Maine Lobster Promotional Council, 64 per cent of us respondents are likely to buy cooked lobster – conveniently packaged or prepared by someone else. But some people and organizations are morally opposed to cooking live lobster and lobsters have become one of the first invertebrates to gain attention in the contentious world animal rights arena.

The worldwide organization People for the Ethical Treatment of Animals, Inc. (PETA) believes that lobsters feel pain and is against killing and eating them; it even offers tips for how to release them back into the ocean safely.

Being
Boiled
Hurts!
LobsterLib.com
P**e**TA

Actress Mary Tyler Moore tried to rescue a lobster from its fate, but she was unable to convince Gladstone's, a California restaurant, to accept $1,000 for Spike, the 65-year-old 7.26 kg (16 lb) lobster they kept in a tank. 'To me, eating a lobster is out of the question', objected Moore in a 1995 advertisement published in a Rockland, Maine newspaper. The ad was part of a protest against the Maine Lobster Festival by Moore and the international group People for the Ethical Treatment of Animals (PETA). 'If we had to drop live pigs or chickens into scalding water, chances are that few of us would eat them. Why should it be any different for lobsters?' (The restaurant decided to keep Spike as a pet.) Other celebrities have voiced outrage about cooking lobsters – from Brigitte Bardot to Sir Paul McCartney.

Global sympathy is increasing, with countries such as Australia, Britain, Canada, Italy, New Zealand, Norway and Scotland considering including lobsters in animal welfare laws even while studies show contradictory results about whether they experience pain. In 2003 Canada, which has one of the world's largest lobster fisheries, considered approving an animal welfare law that would make boiling lobsters a crime.

But so far it appears that only New Zealand, some Australian states and a town in Italy have passed laws to protect this crustacean. The New South Wales 1979 anti-cruelty act covers crustaceans only where they're being prepared for consumption, such as in a restaurant. In 2000 New Zealand enacted an animal welfare law that deemed lobsters 'animals', and made killing them inhumanely an offence.

'Useless torture' is what the town council in Reggio Emilia called boiling live lobster and in 2004 they banned it. Italy, lauded for many similar civic bans, was named 'Progressive Country of the Year' by PETA in the same year. Outlawing the consumption of lobsters is the ultimate goal of the Shellfish Network, a British anti-cruelty organization that proposed legal protection for crustaceans in 2004 with specific steps to decrease their suffering from trap to table, including biodegradable escape panels and individual tubes for shipping. Their suggestions to the UK's Select Committee on Environment, Food and Rural Affairs were rejected because according to the Shellfish Network the committee felt the research didn't show clearly that lobsters felt pain and it was hard to include lobster in a bill without covering all invertebrates. Other protesters have chosen illegal methods, including the Lobster Liberation Front (LLF), a covert activist crusade of individuals that started destroying lobster equipment and freeing lobsters in 2004. They have continued infrequently to sabotage lobster fishing equipment and to liberate lobsters in England, Italy, Scotland, Sweden and Turkey, chronicling their actions in *Bite Back* magazine.

The Norwegians were concerned enough about the possibility of lobsters and other invertebrates experiencing pain when handled by humans that they requested a special report from the Norwegian Scientific Committee for Food Safety. In 2005 the committee reviewed the literature and concluded that 'it appears that most species of invertebrates probably are unable to feel pain, stress and discomfort', and assumed that the ferocious behaviour such as clawing the sides of the pot, tail flapping etc. when lobsters are being boiled is a 'response to noxious stimuli'. They said that an answer to this question was difficult to uncover and recommended more research.

Granting rights to other animals has fuelled the larger debate. It is not such a leap of imagination to see why animals such as the great apes were granted limited rights not to be killed, tortured or abused for the first time in Spain in 2008 – they are our closest biological relatives, after all. It is a much bigger hurdle for some to see why crustaceans should be protected legally. Yet growing numbers have made the leap, as evidenced by the growth of animal rights organizations and legislation. This movement has given rise to new groups such as 'ethical eaters', who want flavoursome, organic food that has been raised compassionately.

Lobster is practically the last food that non-hunting humans routinely kill themselves and then eat. People picking up dinner don't regard themselves as hunters or fishers or people who have to kill what they're going to serve for dinner that night. Although we may shuck and slurp down raw oysters or steam smaller shellfish in our own kitchens, the lobster is closer to a squawking chicken. We can see how alive it really is and its reaction when we cook it. How to kill lobsters humanely is one of the most difficult issues and companies have jumped in with alternatives, echoing nineteenth-century innovators.

5
Killing and Cooking (Humanely)

The quintessential nightmare of attempting to cook lobster at home is portrayed in *Annie Hall*, a 1977 Academy Award-winning American film: Annie's romantic dinner is wrecked when the live lobsters fall to the floor and one escapes, hiding behind the refrigerator. Her boyfriend, played by director and co-writer Woody Allen, wisecracks, 'Maybe if I put a little dish of butter sauce here with a nutcracker, it will run out the other side.' Clearly, cooking live lobster is not for the squeamish. But avoiding the same disaster in your own kitchen is pretty easy. The biggest quandary now is how to cook this crustacean humanely at home. Now there's the chill, kill and grill (or boil) approach; and the stun gun.

Around the world, people buy their lobsters live and there are almost as many ways to kill a lobster as there are to cook it. To see one man's approach visit 'How to Kill a Lobster', Trevor Corson's lobster blog, where he demonstrates how to slay a lobster with a knife in both pictures and narrative. He advises first chilling the lobster in the freezer for about fifteen minutes before humanely dispatching it, but forewarns that this is a delicate manoeuvre that can cause injury to the chef. With the body upside down, you split the body or carapace all the way up through the head with a

sharp knife. Don't worry if the hind legs and tail still flutter –
it is dead. Then cook it right away. A former lobster fisherman, it's obvious that Corson is concerned about the stress
both to the lobster and the chef. But that's just one lobsterman's opinion.

Chilling Works

One lobster scientist, at least, prefers a more direct method.
Dr Robert Bayer simply chills them for about half an hour
and then dunks them in a huge pot of boiling water, probably without salt because, as he explains, he can never get
the proportions right, and cooks them for fifteen to twenty
minutes. Of course, he'd use seawater if it was handy because
it provides 'a unique flavour'. Bayer, who has been studying
the American lobster since about 1976, doesn't kill them
before he cooks them because he's not sure whether it makes
any difference. But he realizes that many people are anxious
about cooking a lobster.

The tail twitch lasts about a minute. That twitch is perhaps the most disturbing part of cooking this cold-blooded
crustacean. Usually the meat we cook at home never moves a
muscle. That alarming twitch is why Bayer decided to decipher ways to shorten the time the tail spasms. This is just the
kind of question the institute, a joint industry-university
effort founded in 1987, is interested in. Bayer and his researchers scrutinized different methods and discovered that
lobsters move the least when they have been chilled in the
freezer or on ice before plunging them into a pot of boiling
water. (Caution: place lobsters on top of the ice, otherwise
they will drown in the unsalted melting water.) Chilling an-
aesthetizes the lobster, and Bayer believes that the shellfish

doesn't register the nosedive into the pot as anything more than a change in temperature. He suggests chilling the lobster for fifteen to thirty minutes in a home freezer until it appears lethargic, which requires one to check it periodically. Another way to reduce the cook's trauma, explains Bayer, is to put the lobster in fresh water; though the lobster does drown, it appears to be going to sleep. One can also rub the top of the body's shell or carapace – down the middle of the back – which some think 'hypnotizes' the lobster, although, as Bayer says, they 'still flap around just as much as ever' when you put them in the boiling water. They die rapidly, he explains, because what there is of a nervous system breaks down very quickly. But he emphasizes that for them to die in seconds, there must be enough water to cover them when submerged in a rolling boil.

According to the Lobster Institute's website, that means filling a big, tall pot about three-quarters full of either salted water (10 ml/95 litres; 2 tbs/1 qt) or seawater. Every lobster needs almost 2.5 litres (about 2½ qt) of water. Drop each lobster into the pot, cover it and then bring it to another boil. Reduce the heat and simmer the hard-shell lobsters for around fifteen (450–570 g/1–1¼ lb) to twenty (750 g/1½ lb) minutes. Cook soft-shell lobsters for three minutes less.

If you believe that crustaceans can feel pain and suffering whether they are cooked or eaten raw, as does Australia's Royal Society for the Prevention of Cruelty to Animals (RSPCA Australia), you'll follow their advice. The length of time required to chill a lobster until it seems anaesthetized depends on the shellfish and the conditions, but they suggest that if the tail or abdomen is moved easily it's safe to assume it is unconscious. Since the lobster's nervous system is decentralized, the RSPCA doesn't advise killing it by stabbing a knife into the head, called head spiking, a technique sometimes used

Lobsters are ideal for grilling, including these spiny lobster tails.

by restaurants and courageous home cooks. Instead they agree with Corson that cutting down through the centre of the body to the tail will quickly destroy the nerves. The RSPCA finds many methods completely unacceptable, frowning on eating live crustaceans, putting them in fresh water or hot or boiling water, and dismembering them (tailing them or chopping off parts of the shellfish, even if they have been chilled). So much for steaming them on the beach.

So now what's the poor lobster cook to do? Convince the lobster to jump into the pot to save the cook the distress of killing it? If you don't want to give up and go to a restaurant, any of these methods will reduce lobster pain and distress.

What Cooks Should Know

Those looking for the most delectable lobster preparation might turn to Boston chef Jasper White, who agrees with Bayer that using ocean water produces 'the briny-sweet taste of the sea', and believes in not crowding a lobster pot. White, author of *Lobster at Home* and one of America's foremost chefs, wants to keep the essence of the shellfish and advises steaming rather than boiling lobsters. In his opinion, the meat is more tender when cooked more slowly with steam and the true flavour is preserved, since the steam doesn't dilute the lobster.

British chef Rick Stein takes a completely different approach to chilling and killing lobster. In his cookbook *Rick Stein's Complete Seafood* he directs the cook to put the lobster in the freezer for two hours to kill it without pain and then boil it in heavily salted water – 150 g/½ cup of salt for every 4.5 litres/10 pints of water. After dropping the lobster in the pot and bringing the water back to a boil, cook 750 g/1½ lb for fifteen minutes and 1.25 kg/2½ lb for twenty minutes.

It's not clear who first came up with the idea of putting a lobster in the freezer to kill it before cooking, but *Larousse Gastronomique*, a proponent of this method, credits the British Universities Federation for Animal Welfare for the inspiration. There is one additional tip that *Larousse* offers: after plunging the lobster head-first into a pot holding even more salted boiling water than previous suggestions (4.5 litres or 1 gallon, 5 qt for each lobster), hold it down with a wooden spoon for at least two minutes.

If you're thinking about eating a dead lobster, think again. Forget cooking any shellfish – crab, clam, lobster, mussel or oyster – that has died before you prepare it. Immediately after death lobsters begin to decay from their digestive system enzymes. So lobsters taste best cooked live. If you're uneasy about cooking one or are in a hurry, you can buy them conveniently cooked or frozen. If you buy a cooked lobster and the meat is like 'soft, woolly flesh', Stein warns, it was cooked after dying.

Let's say you opt for live lobsters to prepare at home. It's vital to purchase vigorous specimens from a trusted source on the same day you plan to cook them. It's obvious that Jasper White lives near the coast because he suggests buying them directly from a lobster boat or a lobster co-op or company found near the ocean, ensuring fresh lobsters. But most of us only find these crustaceans in seafood market tanks filled with artificially salinated and oxidized water; in these conditions lobsters quickly lose their essence. So look for a bustling market that sells a lot of lobsters. White calls supermarkets the last option for procuring these shellfish because the focus usually is not on fresh, high-turnover seafood. If in the tank there is evidence of overcrowding, murky water, algae or dead lobsters, he advises you 'take a stroll over to the meat counter . . . saving lobster for another day', or order them by mail.

Healthy lobsters are frisky, waving their claws and flapping their tails when pulled from the water. Of course, they do this to make killing them even harder. No matter what, avoid the ones with short or algae-covered antennae, lifeless tails or drooping claws. Don't worry about the rubber bands or wooden pegs on the claws of American lobsters – there's no evidence that they affect the taste and it's safer both for cooks and their companions to leave them on. (And, since these lobsters are cannibals, they may try to eat their dinner mates.)

White advocates buying the hardest-shelled lobster. He suggests shaking it tenderly to see if it 'rattles', which indicates that it's soft rather than the preferred meaty texture. But he

A Monhegan Island, Maine lobsterman uses a banding tool to put a protective rubber band around the claw of an American lobster.

admonishes the cook to be flexible in choosing quality over size, especially since he believes lobsters taste best up to 2.25 kg (5 lb). In us the sizes have a nomenclature all their own. The most common are 'chicken lobsters', nicknamed 'chix', weighing about ½ kg (just over a pound), measuring about 8 cm (at least 3¼ in.) from behind the eye socket to the end of the carapace. They tend to be seven to eight years old, having moulted close to 25 times. The most expensive are usually the 'select lobsters', the most sought-after, ranging between 750 g and 1.25 kg (1½ and 2½ lb) and the 'jumbo lobsters' weighing 1.25 kg (2½ lb) and over. Lobster 'culls' – those missing a claw – are usually reasonably priced and ideal for dishes requiring lobster meat. If you want to continue eating lobster, never buy a 'short' lobster under the us legal size of about ½ kg (1 lb); a female lobster that's either berried (where eggs are on the underside of the tail or abdomen) or v-notched (with a v-shaped piece missing from its tail, indicating that it's a female); or a lobster that weighs over five pounds: all are necessary as breeding stock.

How long can you keep a lobster alive out of water, especially if you can't cook it the same day? A common answer is one to two days. Under the best storage conditions, White believes robust ones can survive three to five days, while frail ones may die within a day. Bayer says that it depends on their stage of moult. Although he's not recommending it, sometimes he's kept an older hard-shell lobster in his refrigerator for two weeks. Yet a new soft-shell lobster may survive a day or less, and it's all because of its oxygen-carrying pigments (soft-shelled lobsters are less efficient at extracting oxygen from moisture). It also hinges on how you store them. Bayer recommends moist newspaper or paper towels but preferably dampened with seawater in a refrigerator (although, at a pinch, tap water works). Howard Hillman, author of *The New Kitchen Science*, writes that they can extract oxygen from the moisture that clings to their gills, and should be kept at about 10° C (50° F), ideally on a bed of wet seaweed. Be advised that

The American lobster, nicknamed the Maine lobster, has a pair of dangerous but delicious claws.

Canadian lobstermen wedge pegs in lobsters' claws in Cape John, Nova Scotia, 1930s; wooden pegs were used before they were replaced by rubber bands.

according to Hillman the sweet flavour will fade after one to two days of storage. Bayer recommends the sniff test – a fresh lobster should not smell like anything; otherwise it's not fresh or edible.

Assuming that after storing and killing your lobster, you still want to eat it, where to start? The most formidable part of the American lobster is also the most delectable. The two claws are their biggest defensive weapons that they use to protect their smooth, thin shell. The larger crusher claw can crunch opponents and other shellfish; the smaller is the more manoeuvrable pincer, ripper or cutter claw. Both rip up the food into little pieces that will fit into the lobster's mouth. The tail or substantially muscled abdomen contains firm, delicious meat. When snapped down it can propel a lobster backwards into a rocky crevice at recorded speeds of five metres per second. Flavoursome morsels in the body cavity and in the ten legs are often overlooked even by discerning diners. (Avoid the gills, inedible feather-like strands in the body.)

As with any animal, lobsters also have organs, some with strange names. 'Tomalley' is one of the most prized parts of the lobster, savoured alone for its richness or in flavoursome sauces. But that flavour may come at a price. This mushy green material found in the body cavity, often called the liver, is the lobster's filter and storage centre for environmental toxins including heavy metals, PCBS and pesticide residues. To be precise, it is really a combination of liver, pancreas and digestive tract. In addition to those toxins, another concern, paralytic shellfish poisoning (PSP) or red tide, also produces toxins in the food lobsters eat, such as clams and mussels. As recently as 2008, the American government agency, the FDA, issued health warnings about Atlantic lobsters, saying that high levels of PSP had been discovered in tomalley, usually not affecting the lobster meat. So if you've been looking for an excuse to pass on the mushy green stuff, now you have one.

The roe (only in female lobsters), sometimes called coral after its colour when cooked, is also valued for its intense flavour in sauces and soups. So far there are no warnings on this delicacy. If it is red-pink and hard, it has been overcooked. The coral is found in the body and into the tail. Assuming you can find it, the stomach is not generally eaten but is not poisonous. When American lobsters are cooked, white gooey globs appear in the lobster and water – lobster blood. It's edible but doesn't have much taste, unless dipped in butter, which always makes anything taste better.

The bigger crusher claw (on the left) has larger 'teeth', and the pincer, ripper or cutter claw (on the right) has smaller, sharper 'teeth'.

Whatever their original colour – blue, black, brown, green or violet – lobsters always turn red, or more accurately reddish orange, when they're cooked (apart from the white ones). The heat from cooking releases the yellowish red carotene-like pigment in the shell.

Besides the incomparable lobster flavour, there are many other good reasons to eat lobster meat. There are fewer calories, cholesterol and fat in Atlantic lobster than in skinless white chicken meat, lean beef or poached eggs, but only if you eat it without butter or a sauce. It also contains various healthy vitamins and minerals.

What Some Restaurants Do

If, at this point, you'd opt for eating a lobster killed by someone else, probably in a restaurant, wouldn't you still wonder how they might do the deed? When the New Zealand government in 1999 wanted to uncover how spiny lobsters were killed by the country's restaurants and retailers, they turned to Dr Neville Gregory, an animal physiologist who has spent over thirty years investigating the stunning and slaughter of animals. At the time Gregory was science director for MIR-INZ or the meat industry research institute for New Zealand; he's now the Royal Veterinary College's science director at the University of London. His conclusion: chill spiny lobsters, but with one substantial difference from Bayer – *kill them* before you cook them. Gregory surveyed New Zealand restaurants and retailers to discover how rock lobsters were put to death. He learned that at least eight practices were in use, and that often at least two of them were combined. They include a roster of methods that might have come from a medieval torture manual: boiling, chest spiking, chilling, drowning in tap water, freezing, head spiking between the eyes, splitting the length of the body and tailing or cutting the body from the abdomen (or tail).

Gregory also cited similar methods at Asian restaurants for dispatching lobsters. The crustaceans are variously chilled, spiked in the head or chest or tailed, but the majority are split lengthwise from head to tail and the body is used to display the meat. Death occurs in other ways such as boiling or drowning in fresh water.

Most of the techniques are inhumane, assuming that term is relevant to such primitive creatures. Forget drowning. And tailing and chest spiking do not cause instant loss of consciousness. As well as being inhumane, boiling, drowning and freezing also alter the lobster meat quality, making it chewy, soft or changed in appearance respectively. The best, most merciful method is essentially the same as Corson's: chill them in a refrigerator or freezer at 2°–4° C (35°–40° F), or iced salt water until they are unresponsive (the time this takes depends on their size). This diminishes nerve function and metabolic activity, but apparently not the meat quality. Right after chilling is the safest time to kill a lobster completely and compassionately before cooking, either by splitting it from the head to the beginning of the tail, destroying the body's nerve centres (ganglia), or spiking the head, breaking the main ganglia – both take some skill. According to Gregory, the chill-kill-grill system also provides undamaged lobster meat.

Lobster Killing Machines

Two contraptions take the killing off your hands and produce lobster meat humanely: the Crustastun and the Big Mother Shucker. There's only one glitch – they're either too big or too expensive for the average home cook. But they're a step in the right direction. The inventors of an electronic stun gun, Charlotte and Simon Buckhaven, two barristers, reputedly stopped eating lobster some twenty years ago when they realized the crustaceans were boiled alive. The British couple wanted a humane way to kill lobsters, crabs and crayfish and worked with University of Bristol scientists to design a device, the Crustastun (really a tank), that initially whacks them unconscious and then demolishes their nervous system with 110 volts of electricity in five to ten seconds. Now anyone in a restaurant or at a fishmonger can simply press the button on the single stunner, avoiding provoking the release of stress hormones and preserving the lobsters' flavour and texture.

The Big Mother Shucker weighs over 36,000 kg (80,000 lb). It is a two-storey-high machine that kills lobsters in about two seconds and loosens the meat from the shell – both with high-pressure water – so that it can be hand-shucked. This machine is used in Shucks Maine Lobster plant kitchen and made by Avure Technologies Inc. in Washington State and Sweden. The fresh, raw, all-natural Maine lobster is vacuum-sealed and then pressure-treated again, effectively cold-pasteurizing to give it about a nine-day shelf life. Touting flavour and texture, this mid-coast Maine company ships this convenient form of lobster to other food service providers and some US grocery stores.

Don't kid yourself – cooking a lobster at home is a challenge. But now with the experts' opinions, there are clear steps: chill the lobster first, kill it by splitting head to beginning of the tail (or kill it by freezing it) and then boil or steam it in salted water. And whether you choose to cook a lobster at home or not, there is always frozen lobster sold in grocery stores or on the Web, or prepared in a restaurant. But if we

For about £2,500 Crustastun sells a single 'stun gun' or device that renders a lobster unconscious in less than half a second and kills it within 5–10 seconds with 110 volts of electricity. It is recommended by some animal welfare organizations.

always make that choice, what becomes of the notion of eating a lobster? If diners replace cracking a claw with opening a can or microwaving lobster in a plastic bag, we are in danger of losing one of the last connections between the food we ingest and its origin.

6

The Future of Lobsters

Diamond Jim Brady could devour six to seven lobsters in one sitting. A millionaire with a reputation for a huge appetite and wearing expensive jewellery, James Buchanan Brady reputedly 'ate everything that was set before him – to the sixth and seventh helping', including lobster, during a two-hour shore dinner. Whether this is true or not, Brady was America's 'foremost eater of the Gilded Age', and had the waistline to prove it. He especially liked dining at Rector's, '*the* lobster palace of the period', a pricey, lavish restaurant specializing in lobster that attracted the affluent crowd in New York City in the late nineteenth century. 'When he'd eaten about four portions of the oysters . . . it would be time for his *Lobster Americain* [*sic*]', said owner George Rector, who made it for him in their largest chafing dish. 'And where the recipe called for one lobster, for Diamond Jim I used two – always two of everything.' Brady polished off fresh lobsters as only the self-indulgent wealthy could at the turn of the century, when enormous demand from the east coast canneries was straining lobster fisheries and raising prices.

A 1902 *New York Times* article predicted the imminent annihilation of the *Homarus* lobster, anticipating 'the day when the lobster will be as rare as the buffalo', and pointed

Women in Pictou, Nova Scotia are removing the lobster meat from the shell in what was locally known as Magee's lobster factory, a Fred Magee, Ltd cannery, in the 1930s.

the finger at the canneries. Those on North America's east coast were 'decimating them so rapidly that all authorities agree that their extinction is only a matter of a brief period', continued the anonymous author of the article. The estimated 1,440 canneries on Newfoundland's coast shipped worldwide 33,000 cases the previous year, each filled with 48 one-pound tins of the shellfish using over 9 million lobsters, and worth almost $400,000. Including those trapped for the local population, an estimated 12 million lobsters were caught in Newfoundland's waters in 1901. Plus there were 23 canneries in Maine. The journalist speculated that the combination of endless desire for lobster from careless canners and trampled regulations would speed the death of the shellfish. The diminished supply and additional regulations eventually put the canneries out of business and allowed lobster stocks to make a comeback during the rest of the century.

Sizeable catches for both Canada and the US at the beginning of this century seem to support the notion of a recovery. While you won't find giant lobsters on the Atlantic beach anymore, it's no longer their proportions but their quantity and price that count. The worldwide lobster industry for both the clawed and clawless varieties is now worth billions of dollars annually, and North America is a large part of it. Just the Atlantic catch is astounding. In 2008 the two biggest haulers, Canada and the US, brought in more than 55,000 metric tons valued at over £300 million and almost 42,000 metric tons valued at over £240 million respectively. Maine, the largest lobster-producing American state, which reached an all-time high in 2006, hauled in almost 31,000 metric tons valued at almost £144 million in 2008. In 2006–7, Australia's rock lobster production was 13,698 metric tons, worth over £240,000.

With such hefty numbers, there is growing concern about the long-term sustainability of this adaptable species, especially since more of the mature breeding stock are caught for the dinner table. Unfortunately, there is no way to accurately measure the lobster population other than by counting what is caught, also called landings. As seen throughout history, record hauls do not predict the future. They may even be the bellwether of future calamity. Consider those statistics the first clue. And two unexpected and unexplained lobster tragedies.

In September 1999 a calamitous lobster die-off in Long Island Sound destroyed a £60 million industry that was riding the crest of record catches. Temperature seems to have played a pivotal part. The residue of Hurricane Floyd increased the water temperature, eliminating the necessary oxygen from it. But Diane F. Cowan, a research scientist and founder of The Lobster Conservancy, suspected there were additional reasons for the tragedy. She suggested that the combination of vigorous harvesting that depleted the existing lobster population, the storm's intense rain that flooded the Sound and recent applications of mosquito pesticides resulted in a lobster environment suddenly full of toxic waste. The coast was also becoming more inhospitable to lobsters with the slow, steady escalation of sewage dumped in the Sound, industrial activities that raised water temperatures and pipelines that created obstacles to healthy breeding. Lobsters require 'waters . . . [that] are oxygen-rich, cool and relatively devoid of contamination', explained Cowan in her 2006 *New York Times* article. She warned this could happen again just as easily. Can these ancient, successful shellfish withstand such environmental changes at the same time as being overfished?

Lobster landings in 2003 plunged to their lowest level in almost three decades in one of Canada's most fertile lobster habitats, the Northumberland Strait. These hospitable waters lie between New Brunswick, Nova Scotia and Prince Edward Island. It is unclear why the steady decline suddenly accelerated (luckily it's the only place north of Cape Cod where this has happened), but lobstermen jest that the area should be renamed Dire Strait. According to biologists, it could be a normal cycle in lobster stocks or because fishers unwittingly snatch the females just before they lay eggs. The list of possibilities contains the usual suspects including industrial pollution and warmer waters. Some blame the more sophisticated equipment such as depth sounders and power haulers, and the bigger, better traps that appeared in the 1980s when the decline began. Others blame scallop draggers who disturb the lobsters' terrain, or summer poachers.

Regulations Protect Lobsters

Some lobster poachers do get caught. Wayne Miller of For-
tune, Canada was fined $2,500 in December 2007 for possess-
ing five female v-notched lobsters after a dockside inspection.
V-notched lobsters have had a triangular sliver carved out of
their tail flipper by fishermen, marking them as good breeders
and supposedly ensuring that they may not be harvested for
life. Miller was one of four punished for keeping the repro-
ductive stock.

Cheats like Miller are just one of many reasons for the
depleted lobster fishery. Shady harvesters will sell 'scrubs', the
nickname of female lobsters whose abdomens (what we call
tails) have been scrubbed of eggs; others will sell 'shorts' –
lobsters that do not meet the minimum size limit. Others trap
the shellfish outside legal harvesting limits and sell them on
the black market, which excludes those lobsters from the
annual fishery counts and undermines sustainability efforts.
Canada provides more than half of the world's supply of live
and processed hard-shell Atlantic lobster to consumers in 55
countries from America to Australia to Vietnam, and obvi-
ously wants to preserve this billion-dollar seafood export.

In the 1870s both Canada and the United States began
regulating the lobster industry by setting minimum legal
sizes for the carapace. The carapace is what diners call the
'body', and is measured with a special brass gauge starting at
the lobster's eye socket down to where the shell meets the
'tail' or abdomen. Canada was the first to establish the minimum size, which now varies for its individual lobster fishery
areas. (Canada allows smaller lobsters for their influential
canning industry.) Maine was only a year behind them and
today its legal minimum length is 83 mm (3¼ in., about 1¼
lb), as it is in most other states. Although the minimum limit

Lobster eggs are attached to the female *Homarus*'s tail with strands of glue from her cement glands. The eggs are roughly the size of a tiny raspberry segment, hence the term 'berried female', and take about nine months to hatch.

is ubiquitous in North America, this restriction continues to be controversial because scientists have suggested a slightly higher minimum that gives these crustaceans more time to reach sexual maturity and produce offspring. The maximum carapace length is another measure that scientists support in order to protect the brood stock, but this has not achieved widespread support. The exceptions are Maine, which implemented this restriction in 1933, and parts of Canada; but not all American states have followed suit to date. Today Maine's legal length is 127 mm (5 in., about 3–4 lb). Both countries unquestioningly support safeguarding egg-bearing or berried females, and have made it illegal to keep them. Although still only voluntary in Canada, the us requires that their tails be v-notched before they are released so they can be easily identified as productive females. Tail notching has spread to other countries including Ireland in the 1990s. Other methods have been used by different countries to regulate the lobster catch, including closed or staggered fishing seasons, specifying trap design and limiting the number of boats, licences and traps. It was the work of Francis Hobart Herrick, a significant American lobster biologist, who introduced many of these scientifically based recommendations to sustain the 'king of the crustacean class' in his books in the late 1880s.

With or without controls, lobstering is notoriously inefficient and that helps prevent some overfishing. Neither trapping nor diving is highly productive. Undersized lobsters can leave through the required escape hatches in traps but they're not the only ones. Even edible-sized specimens can crawl in and back out again through the normal entryway –

This Maine lobsterman is using a brass measuring gauge to ensure the lobster meets the minimum size limits. Lobsters are measured from the eye socket to the beginning of the tail. The US and Canada have different minimum sizes.

The yellow hatches on these traps sitting on the dock at Owl's Head, Maine in 2004 make it easier for undersized lobsters to escape.

they've been videotaped doing it. And once a lobster is in the trap, it will protect the bait, fighting off others trying to enter and unexpectedly limiting the number caught in each trap.

A pristine Maine cove picturesquely cluttered with multi-coloured lobster buoys that are connected to traps on the sea floor is a standard postcard scene. But imagine what the sea floor of lobstering grounds must look like. Some experts estimate that there are 2.5 million lobster pots off the Maine coast. That postcard view may change. These lobstermen are facing new pressure from environmentalists to protect the remaining North Atlantic right whales at the same time as feeling the pressures of plummeting lobster prices, and soaring bait and fuel prices. Now the fishers may even be asked to reduce the number of traps, perhaps at the same time being required to use new equipment, like the sinking ropes that connect traps on the sea floor to prevent whale entanglement. Not that the ocean bottom congested with traps couldn't use a little traffic management. Perhaps growing lobsters on farms will offer wild lobsters some additional relief.

Preserving the Lobster

Even if we wanted to give wild lobsters a break, it may take a miracle for farmed lobsters to appear on dinner plates. The elusive dream of growing lobsters commercially has mirrored the popularity and demand for this revered shellfish, waxing and waning for almost 150 years – as has the governmental funding of research for commercial production. Its potential is the direct result of scientists determined to decipher lobster biology enough to raise them for human consumption. The researchers began with the intention of restocking lobster populations that had declined substantially – discovering how to raise baby lobsters in hatcheries from eggs taken from wild females and then releasing the juveniles into the ocean. Today this is the easiest and most common method of culturing *Homarus* lobsters, and a serious 'stock enhancement' or 'sea ranching' effort is under way in Canada. A second, more challenging, technique is to hatch, rear and grow lobsters to market size, which is happening now in Norway. Scientific sleuths have learned how to produce eggs from female lobsters grown in captivity. The third course, or 'product enhancement', has been to catch smaller lobsters and increase their size enough to sell them.

The popular spiny lobster is also in much demand but aquaculture is more difficult. Scientists have been accumulating data about its biology and conducting experiments for years. In particular, Australia, Japan and New Zealand have been very much involved. There have been some trial farms but there has been little commercial interest and, when there

Homarus lobsters go through many stages of development but as this picture shows, even at a very young stage they look like adults.

is, it's often kept confidential for competitive reasons. One reason that aquaculture is difficult is because spiny lobsters have a more complex life cycle than North Atlantic lobsters, so it takes longer for them to grow to commercial size, requiring five to eleven years to mature. Another is that they moult many times during these early stages and can break their fragile spines if they bump up against anything, including a tank wall. They also need proper feed, cost-effective hatchery technology and a business that's willing to take a risk to produce them.

'Only about 8 species have been grown through their entire larval development to settlement [taking up residence on the mussel ropes or seaweed, for instance] and for only a couple of species has this been achieved in significant numbers', says Dr John D. Booth, retired from New Zealand's National Institute of Water and Atmospheric Research.

Even so, he believes a few spiny lobster species seem promising: the Japanese spiny lobster (*Panulirus japonicus*), the ornate spiny lobster (*P. ornatus*, from northern Australia) and the eastern packhorse rock lobster (*Sagmariasus verreauxi*, from southern Australia).

It makes sense that the Japanese spiny lobster, caught along the Japanese coasts, is so promising, according to Dr Sheila Patek, assistant professor at the University of Massachusetts in Amherst. The Japanese began the experimental hatching and rearing of Japan's spiny lobster in 1899. It took almost ninety years before they were able to raise them to the 'one centimetre bug' size or 'puerulus' stage. In Patek's opinion the Japanese aquaculture scientists/biologists 'have been really good at mimicking the natural environment – attending to every single detail'. But who knows how long it may be until they are mass-producing lobsters? In the meantime experiments continue in India, Thailand and Vietnam, among others, with wild juvenile lobsters being caught and raised in sea cages to market size.

Attending to the rock lobster fishery may be more important today than aquaculture. The different species are managed throughout the world in a variety of different ways – from size and total catch limits, to quotas, to limited entry into the commercial fishery, to traps with escape hatches for small shellfish and other gear requirements. Even commercial divers and recreational fishers may have restrictions.

Growing Lobsters

Fisherman Ron Cormier helped seed baby lobsters in the Gulf of St Lawrence. His boat, the *Patrick*, carried about 75,000 tiny crustaceans in a grey plastic water tank a couple of miles off the coast of New Brunswick. Cormier slowly opened the tank valve that was attached to a weighted blue hose, about 5 cm in diameter (about 2 in.), that plummeted to the sea floor, delivering the baby lobsters right to their new home via gravity. This method avoids the risk of predators gobbling them up as they swim down to the safety of the rocky crevices and possibly making it more likely they'll end up on a human's plate.

Cormier, a fisherman for 25 years, is part of a group of about 1,500 Canadian lobstermen in the Maritime Fishermen's Union (MFU) who in 2002 helped start an experimental non-profit hatchery in Shippagan, New Brunswick, run by Homarus, Inc. Cormier and lobstermen like him have been worried about the puzzling slump in catches or landings off Prince Edward Island in the south-western Gulf of St Lawrence. It is an enormous contrast to the late 1980s and early 1990s when the area produced historic landings. Cormier, then president of the union, knew lobster fishers had to do something to increase the lobster stock and Homarus would produce both juvenile lobsters and a simple hatchery technology so the fishermen's groups could support their own local seeding ventures. Since 2002 the Homarus hatchery has grown and seeded almost 780,000 lobsters and has the capacity to produce up to 300,000 to 500,000 larvae yearly, according to Martin Mallet, director of the Canadian non-profit research and development subsidiary of MFU. They have increased the survival rate of juvenile lobsters grown from the larvae of wild, egg-laden females through improvements in the larvae tanks, feed and aeration systems. Mallet describes this form of lobster aquaculture as sea ranching, and wants the seeding efforts to expand the number of lobsters.

But the main question about every attempt to increase the lobster population is whether or not it works. The Canadians have tackled this issue too. One positive sign is that 'our research shows that seeded stage IV [baby lobsters] do stay the area where they have been seeded', wrote Mallet. They also release up to 100,000 lobsterlings at each of their experimental sites and they're seeing more lobsters in two out of three of the sites. Even if 5 per cent survive they'll be happy.

Fiona, the spotted orange and yellow lobster caught off Prince Edward Island in 2009, near the Homarus seedings, is not one from their hatchery. So how would consumers or lobster fishers know if one was? Right now, they don't look any different from those hatched in the wild. One of the most promising methods of identification may be to change the lobster's shell colour, giving it a 'natural tag'. Scientists have produced different-coloured lobsters – blue, orange, red, white and multi-coloured – through regulated matings. The advantage is that these colours are so rare that they only show up in one in 30 million lobsters or more. Don't worry – their shells still turn red when cooked (unless they're white).

Apparently Great Britain, Norway and Scotland have shown that not only do these lobster babies live after they're liberated but they also can reproduce, perhaps rejuvenating the wild lobster pool. This is an especially crucial strategy when almost an entire lobster stock has collapsed as is the case in Norway where there continues to be a strong market demand and rising prices. Sea ranching of *Homarus gammarus* lobsters in Norway is now a licensed commercial industry that may be successful if their hatcheries can produce heaps of inexpensive and superior juveniles. Rather than wait about five to seven years for hatchery-reared lobsters to mature in the wild, the Norwegians have decided to grow a plate-sized European lobster in less than three years in a facility on land rather than in the ocean.

Rick Stein, TV chef and millionaire restaurateur, was worried about getting enough European lobsters for diners in seafood restaurants and hotels. With *H. gammarus* only supplying about 3 per cent of the global catch and the increasing demand for the luxurious shellfish, he had good reason to worry. Seafood preparation is a speciality of Stein, 61, who started his first restaurant in the North Cornwall harbour village of Padstow, nicknamed 'Padstein'. Stein, who also has hotels, a cookery school and a television show in the United Kingdom, hopes to have a steady supply of plate-sized lobster from the Norwegian commercial lobster farming company Norsk Hummer AS. In 2008 Stein teamed up with Norsk Hummer and seven other partners in an effort to produce the 300–400 g European lobster. Norsk Hummer makes a strong partner for this enterprise since much of the knowledge we have today about reproducing Atlantic lobsters comes from the Scandinavians, especially the Norwegians, who were renowned for their early fish hatcheries.

How Consumers Can Help

Cormier encourages people to eat lobsters, but he cautions consumers to beware of poachers who sell undersized or berried female lobsters, perhaps even out of season. Cormier also recommends eating the 570 g to almost 1 kg (1 ¼–2 lb) lobster, which protects the brood stock but also because he believes the larger ones are tougher and not as tasty.

Even if lobster stocks are well managed with regulations, 'they're clearly pushed very hard,' says Patek. Her specific recommendation: if consumers are going to eat lobsters then the bare minimum they can do is to make sure the lobster is a legal size and 'know where they're from'. (She also advocates the support of marine reserves where lobsters can find refuge, such as Australia's Great Barrier Reef.) So start with fishers, harvesters and shippers who use eco-friendly, sustainable methods.

How do consumers know who to buy from and which species of lobsters are in danger? Your fishmonger or restaurant server probably won't know. Your best bet is to look for the blue and white eco-label from the Marine Stewardship Council (MSC), an independent, non-profit, global fishery organization that combats overfishing and harmful harvesting methods by certifying sustainable and well-managed, wild-capture fisheries. Already, it vouches for the Eastern Canada offshore lobster, the Western Australia rock lobster, and a couple of Norway lobster (*Nephrops norvegicus*) fisheries off Scotland's coast, 'Stornoway nephrops trawl' and 'Loch Torridon nephrops creel'. The red rock fishery in Baja California, Mexico was the first Latin American and first community-based, developing-world artisanal fishery validated by MSC, and is being reassessed. More than five hundred rural fishermen from ten villages on the Baja California peninsula participate. Additional lobster fisheries are being assessed – Maine lobster trap fishery (sponsored by Shucks Maine Lobster), Normandy & Jersey lobster located in Western Europe, Sian Ka'an and Banco Chinchorro Biosphere Reserves on Mexico's Yucatan Peninsula, North East England lobster pot fishery, Tristan da

The nonprofit, independent Marine Stewardship Council, a global organization, guarantees that certain seafood including some lobster is certified as sustainable. Look for the blue and white ecolabel.

Chunha rock lobster, which is a British Overseas Territory in the South Atlantic Ocean, and a handful of Nephrops fisheries. Some grocery stores have replaced live lobster with frozen lobster meat, but if it doesn't have the blue eco-label of certification from the Marine Stewardship Council it may not have been sustainably caught.

Your second best step is to use a list from various websites that identify some of the best and worst choices of edible seafood including lobster. The Blue Ocean Institute's *Guide to Ocean Friendly Seafood* highlights fish with the msc's blue label. Other possibilities are the us Environmental Defense Fund's *Pocket Seafood Selector* or the Monterey Bay Aquarium's *Seafood Watch Pocket Guide*.

Though most of us don't eat lobsters the way Brady did, we humans always seem to want more of the crustacean. There is pressure on all sides. The sustainable-food movement bolsters the desire for wild seafood. That intensified market demand along with decreased prices and increased costs press lobstermen to catch more. Fishers, scientists, conservation groups, environmentalists and government officials are still at odds over how to save this revered shellfish, but careful management is essential. However, sustainability lies in our hands too. We may not leave piles of shells for our descendants to uncover, festivals aside, but we do want them to have the pleasure of eating a lobster. Don't we?

Recipes

Historical Recipes

Boiled Spiny Lobster
—from Apicius, late fourth to fifth century AD:
translated by Chris Grocock and Sally Grainger,
*Apicius, a Critical Edition With an Introduction
and English Translation*, 2006

Serve [boiled lobster] well with cumin sauce: pepper, lovage,
parsley, dry mint, plenty of cumin, honey, vinegar, *liquamen* [salty
fish sauce]; if you want add *folium* [cinnamon] and *malabathrum*
[cinnamon].

Another Spiny Lobster Recipe
—from Apicius, late fourth to fifth century AD:
translated by Chris Grocock and Sally Grainger,
*Apicius, a Critical Edition With an Introduction
and English Translation*, 2006

You make forcemeat from its tail like this: first remove the harmful leaf parts [of *folium nociuum*] and boil it. Then chop the meat
and make a forcemeat with *liquamen* [salty fish sauce], pepper
and eggs.

To pickle Lobsters
—from Robert May,
The Accomplisht Cook, or the Art and Mystery of Cookery, 1671

Boil them in vinegar, white-wine, and salt; being boild take them up and lay them by, then have some bay-leaves, rosemary tops, winter savory, tyme, large mace, and whole pepper: boil these foresaid materials all together in the liquor with the lobsters and some whole cloves; being boild barrel them in a vessel that will but just contain them, pack them close, pour the liquid to them, herbs, spices, and some lemon-peels, close up the head of the kegg or firkin, and keep them for your use; when you serve them, serve them with the spices, herbs, peels, and some of the liquor or pickle.

Lobsters to pot
—from Anne Gibbons Gardiner,
Mrs Gardiner's Receipts from 1763

Take the [meat] out of the Claws and Belly of a boiled Lobster, which put in a marble mortar with two blades of Mace, a little white Pepper and a little Salt, with a Lump of butter, of the Size of an Egg; beat them all together untill they come to a Paste, of which put one half into your Pot; then take the meat out of the Tail part, and lay that in the middle of your Pot over which lay the remaining half of your Paste; then press it down close and pour clarified Butter over it, a quarter of an Inch thick.

Lobster Pie, another way
—from Anne Gibbons Gardiner,
Mrs Gardiner's Receipts from 1763

Boil two Lobsters, take out the Tails which cut in two Lengthwise, and take out the Gut; then cut the Tail in four pieces and lay them in a Dish. Bruise the Bodies and the Claws and take out all the Meat, which chop together, and season it with Pepper, Salt, and two or three Spoonsfull of Vinegar; then melt half a pound of good, fresh Butter, and stir all together, with the Crumbs of Bread rolled small in a clean Cloth. Lay this over the Tails and bake it in a slow oven.

To roast Lobsters
—from Mrs Hannah Glasse,
The Art of Cookery, Made Plain and Easy, 1805

Boil your lobsters, then lay them before the fire, and baste them with butter till they have a fine froth. Dish them up with plain melted butter in a cup. This is as good a way to the full as roasting them, and not half the trouble.

To make a fine Dish of Lobsters
—from Mrs Hannah Glasse,
The Art of Cookery, Made Plain and Easy, 1805

Take three lobsters, boil the largest as above, and froth it before the fire. Take the other two boiled, and butter them as in the foregoing receipt. Take the two body shells, heat them hot, and fill them with the buttered meat. Lay the large lobster in the middle, and the two shells on each side; and the two great claws of the middle lobster at each end; and the four pieces of chines of the two lobsters broiled, and laid on each end. This, if nicely done makes a pretty dish.

Lobster Sauce
—from Mrs Hannah Glasse,
The Art of Cookery, Made Plain and Easy, 1805

Take a fine hen lobster, take out all the spawn, and bruise it in a mortar very fine, with a little butter; then take all the meat out of the claws and tail, and cut it in small square pieces; put the spawn and meat in a stew-pan with a spoonful of anchovy liquor, and one spoonful of catchup, a blade of mace, a piece of a stick of horse-radish, half a lemon, a gill of gravy, a little butter rolled in flour, just enough to thicken it; put in half a pound of butter nicely melted, boil it gently up for six or seven minutes; take out the horseradish, mace, and lemon, and squeeze the juice of the lemon into the sauce; just simmer it up, and then put it in your boats.

Lobster Salad
—from Mrs Lydia Maria Child, *The American Frugal Housewife*, 1832

The meat of one lobster is extracted from the shell, and cut up fine. Have fresh hard lettuce cut up very fine; mix it with the lobster. Make a dressing, in a deep plate, of the yolks of four eggs cut up, a gill of sweet oil, a gill of vinegar, half a gill of mustard, half a teaspoonful of cayenne, half a teaspoonful of salt; all mixed well together. To be prepared just before eaten.

Boiled Lobster
—from Miss Catharine Esther Beecher,
Miss Beecher's Domestic Receipt Book, 1846

These must never be cooked after they are dead. Put them alive into boiling water and boil them till the small joints come off easily.

Stewed Lobster
—from C. I. Hood & Co., *Hood's Combined Cook Books*, 1875–85

Cut the lobster in pieces about an inch square. Place them in a stew pan, and over them pour a cup of water; put in butter the size of an egg; pepper and salt to the taste. Mix also with the green dressing of the lobster, and stir it about ten minutes over the fire. Just before taking off, add two wineglasses of port of sherry. Let it scald, but not boil.

118

Deviled Lobster
—from Mrs Mary F. Henderson,
Practical Cooking and Dinner Giving, 1877

[Deviled lobster] is made in the same way as deviled crab, merely substituting the lobster for the crab, and adding a grating of nutmeg to the seasoning. In boiling lobsters and crabs, they are sufficiently cooked when they assume a bright-red color. Too much boiling renders them tough.

[Deviled crab – When the crabs are boiled, take out the meat and cut it into small pieces (dice); clean well the shells. To six ounces of crab meat, mix two ounces of bread-crumbs, two hard-boiled eggs chopped, the juice of half a lemon, Cayenne pepper and salt. Mix all with cream or cream sauce, or, what is still better, a Bechamel sauce . . . Fill the shells with the mixture, smooth the tops, sprinkle over sifted bread-crumbs, and color it in a quick oven.]

Lobsters, Fricasséed, or au Béchamel (Entrée)
—from Eliza Acton, *Modern Cookery, for Private Families*, 1018

Take the flesh from the claws and tails of two moderate-sized lobsters cut it into small scallops or dice; heat it slowly quite through in about three quarters of a pint of good white sauce or *béchamel*; and serve it when it is at the point of boiling, after having stirred briskly to it a little lemon-juice just as it is taken from the fire. The coral, pounded and mixed gradually with a few spoonsful of the sauce, should be added previously. Good shin of beef stock made without vegetables . . . , and somewhat reduced by quick boiling, if mixed with an equal proportion of cream, and thickened with arrow-root, will answer extremely well in a general way for this dish, which is most excellent if well made. The sauce should never be thin; nor more than sufficient in quantity to just cover the fish. For a second course dish, only as much must be used as will adhere to the fish, which after being heated should be laid evenly into the shells, which ought to be split quite through the centre of the backs in their entire length, without being broken or divided at the joint, and nicely cleaned. When thus arranged, the lobster may be thickly covered with well dried, fine, pale fried crumbs of bread, or with unfried ones, which must then be equally moistened with clarified butter, and browned with a salamander. A small quantity of salt, mace, and cayenne, may be required to finish the flavouring of either of these preparations.

[Also used for Acton's 'Common Lobster Patties': Prepare the fish for these as directed for fricasséed lobster, Chapter II, increasing a little the proportion of sauce. Fill the patty-cases with the mixture quite hot, and serve immediately.]

Lobster Butter
—from Eliza Acton, *Modern Cookery, for Private Families*, 1878

Pound to the smoothest possible paste the coral of one or two fresh hen lobsters, mix with it about an equal proportion of fresh firm butter, and a moderate seasoning of mace and cayenne, with a little salt if needed. Let the whole be thoroughly blended, and set aside in a cool larder, or place it over ice until it is sufficiently firm to be made into pats. Serve it garnished with curled parsley, or with any light foliage which will contrast well with its brilliant color. The coral may be rubbed through a fine sieve before it is put into the mortar, and will then require but little pounding.

Lobster Chowder
—from *Godey's Lady's Book and Magazine*, 1881

Lobster
Three crackers
Butter
Salt
Cayenne
One quart of milk

Cut the lobster not fine; pound the crackers very fine and mix with the lobster liver, put in butter, size of a small egg, little salt and Cayenne; work this well together, boil the milk and pour gradually on the paste, stirring all the time; then add the lobster and boil up at once.

Scalloped Lobster
—from Mary Johnson Lincoln,
Mrs Lincoln's Boston Cook Book, 1889

Season *one pint* of *lobster*, cut into dice, with *salt*, *pepper*, and *cayenne*. Mix with *one cup* of *cream sauce* . . . ; fill the lobster shells, using the tail shells of two lobsters. Cover the meat with *cracker crumbs*, moistened with *melted butter*. Bake till the crumbs are brown. Put the two shells together on a platter, with the tail ends out, to look like a long canoe. Lay the small claws over the side to represent oars. Garnish with *parsley*. The lobster may also be served in scallop shells.

Curried Lobster
—from Mary Johnson Lincoln,
Mrs Lincoln's Boston Cook Book, 1889

Make a *curry sauce* . . . ; and warm the diced lobster in the sauce.

[Curry sauce—Cook *one tablespoonful* of *chopped onion* in *one tablespoonful* of *butter* five minutes. Be careful not to burn it. Mix *one tablespoonful* of *curry powder* with *two tablespoonfuls* of *flour*, and stir it into the butter. Add *one pint* of *hot milk* gradually, and stir as directed for white sauce.]

Lobster, Provençal Style
(*Homard à la Provençale*)
—from Charles Ranhofer (former chef of Delmonico's),
The Epicurean, 1894

Divide into equal pieces two medium sized raw lobster tails, season them with salt and mignonette, and sauté them in oil over a very hot fire, turning them round so that they color nicely on both sides. Mince up very finely eight ounces of onions, cutting them first in halves, and suppressing the root and stalk, put them in with the lobster with salt, pepper, mignonette, a bunch of parsley, garnished with thyme and bay leaf, half a pint of tomato sauce . . . , and four spoonfuls of burnt brandy, boil a few minutes; take out the pieces of lobster, strain the sauce through a sieve, and reduce it over a brisk fire with half a bottleful of white wine, despumate the sauce, and when nearly reduced, put back the lobster, season to taste, and serve.

Lobster à la Newberg or Delmonico
(*Homard à la Newberg ou à la Delmonico*)
—from Charles Ranhofer (former chef of Delmonico's),
The Epicurean, 1894

Cook six lobsters each weighing about two pounds in boiling salted water for twenty-five minutes. Twelve pounds of live lobster when cooked yields from two to two and a half pounds of meat and three to four ounces of lobster coral. When cold detach the bodies from the tails and cut the latter into slices, put them into a sautoir, each piece lying flat and add hot clarified butter; season with salt and fry lightly on both sides without colouring; moisten to their height with good raw cream; reduce quickly to half and then add two or three spoonfuls of Madeira wine; boil the liquid once more only, then remove and thicken with a thickening of egg-yolks and raw cream . . . Cook without boiling, incorporating a little cayenne and butter; warm it up again without boiling, tossing the lobster lightly, then arrange the pieces in a vegetable dish and pour the sauce over.

Lobster Bisque

—from Fannie Merritt Farmer,
The Boston Cooking-School Cook Book, 1896

2 lb. lobster
2 cups cold water
4 cups milk
¼ cup butter
¼ cup flour
1 ½ teaspoons salt
Few grains of cayenne

Remove meat from lobster shell. Add cold water to body bones and tough end of claws, cut in pieces; bring slowly to boiling point, and cook twenty minutes.

Drain, reserve liquor, and thicken with butter and flour cooked together. Scald milk with tail meat of lobster, finely chopped; strain and add to liquor. Season with salt and cayenne; then add tender claw meat, cut in dice, and body meat. When coral is found in lobster, wash, wipe, force through fine strainer, put in a mortar with butter, work until well blended, then add flour, stir into soup. If a richer soup is desired, White Stock may be used in place of water.

Modern Recipes

Grilled Crayfish (Rock Lobster)

—with the permission of Magdaleen van Wyk, *The Complete South African Cookbook*, 2007, published by Struik Lifestyle

2 raw crayfish
25 ml (2 tablespoons) butter, melted
lemon juice mixed with melted butter
1 ml (¼ teaspoon) salt
1 ml (¼ teaspoon) pepper
Garnish: finely chopped parsley

Serves 2; Prep time 20 min.; Cooking time 10 min.

1. With a sharp knife, split each crayfish down the centre of its underside, removing the black vein from the tail and the sac from beneath the head.
2. Brush each half with melted butter and place on an oiled grid.
3. Place under the grill, 100 mm away from the direct heat, brushing continually with melted butter, until the meat is white and opaque, about 10 minutes.
4. Season with salt and pepper and serve at once with the lemon juice mixture and parsley sprinkled over the tails.

Note: The crayfish can also be grilled over coals.

Baked Lobster Tail Soufflé (South Africa)

8 servings, Main Dish

Cooking the lobster:
In a large pot, submerge eight 6-ounce African rock lobster tails in lukewarm tap water. Add 1 tablespoon salt and half a lemon, cut in wedges. Bring to a boil and simmer slowly with the lid on for 5 minutes. Turn off the flame and leave lobsters in the water for 30 minutes, then drain.

When cooled, cut the meat out from the underside of the tail, conserving the shell. Reserve the shells. Slice the meat into 8 similar pieces and put in a one-gallon bowl.

White Sauce:
Melt 1 tablespoon butter. Stir in 1 tablespoon flour, ½ teaspoon salt, ⅛ teaspoon white pepper. Gradually stir in ½ cup/110 ml milk or light cream. Heat and stir until thickened. Cool.

Blend into White Sauce:
2 cups/ 350 g ripe honeydew melon, peeled and
cut into ¾-inch (2-cm) dice
½ cup/ 25 g dry breadcrumbs
½ cup/ 110 ml white sauce (see recipe above)
1 tablespoon curry powder
1 teaspoon paprika

Fold in 5 egg whites beaten stiff. Using a spatula, fill the lobster tail shells with this mixture, making a rounded mound in each tail.

Place the tails on a baking sheet and bake at 220°C/425°F for about 10 minutes until golden brown. Avoid overcooking. Serve with Rice Bujambura.

Lobster Cantonese/Yue Shi Chao Long Xia

6 servings, Main Dish

4 live lobsters, 1½–2 pounds (700–900g) each
½ lb (450 g) ground pork

Pork Marinade:
2 teaspoons soy sauce
1 tablespoon sherry
1 teaspoon water
½ teaspoon sesame oil

2 tablespoons peanut, safflower or corn oil

Minced Seasonings:
2 tablespoons fermented black beans, rinsed, drained
and minced
2 tablespoons minced garlic
1 tablespoon minced scallions/spring onions
1 tablespoon minced fresh root ginger
1 stalk finely minced celery

Lobster Sauce:
1 cup/ 225 ml chicken broth
2½ tablespoons soy sauce
2 tablespoons sherry
1 teaspoon sesame oil
1 teaspoon sugar
¼ teaspoon freshly ground black pepper

Thickener:
1 tablespoon water
1½ teaspoons cornstarch

2 large eggs, lightly beaten
1 tablespoon minced scallion greens/spring onions

Chill lobsters for 15 to 30 minutes in a home freezer until they appear lethargic. (Do not freeze them to death.) Cut each lobster in half using a very sharp large chef's knife starting where the tail meets the body all the way up through the head and then back down through the tail. Take the stomach (which is close to the mouth) out of the head; then cut off and throw out the tip of the head with the eyes and the antennae. Take out the intestinal tract, and cut off and toss out the legs along with the intestinal tract. Cut the body including the shell into pieces about 2 inches (5 cm) square.

Chop the ground pork until light and separated, put it into a mixing bowl and gently blend with the pork marinade.

Pour the oil into a heated wok and heat until very hot. Add the minced seasonings, and stir-fry until aromatic, perhaps 10 seconds. Add the ground pork and stir-fry, separating the meat and cooking until the colour changes or for about a minute. Increase flame to high heat. Add the lobster pieces, and stir-fry for about 1 minute. Add the lobster sauce, and bring to a boil. Cook covered for about 3 minutes over high heat. Take off the lid, and drizzle in the thickener, stirring continually to prevent lumps. Once the sauce has thickened, switch off the heat, and gradually add the beaten eggs down the side of the wok. Stir briefly, and pour the contents onto a platter. Scatter the minced scallion greens over top, and serve at once.

Lobster Thermidor

1–2 servings

Chill a live lobster for 15 to 30 minutes in a home freezer until it appears lethargic. (Do not freeze it to death.) Cut the lobster in half, starting where the tail meets the body, all the way up through the head and then back down through the tail. Take out the gills (inedible feather-like strands) from the carcass. Crack the shell of the claws. Lightly salt the lobster halves, drizzle with oil and roast in a preheated oven at 220°C (425°F) until translucent or about 15–20 minutes. Take out the meat from the tail and claws and cut into ⅛ to ¼ inch (3–5 mm) cubes.

Prepare a very thick béchamel or cream sauce:

2 tablespoons butter
2 tablespoons flour
½ teaspoon salt
⅛ teaspoon pepper
⅛ teaspoon nutmeg
2 cups/450 ml milk
2 eggs

Make a stock with equal parts of meat juices, fish fumet and white wine. Add chervil, chopped shallots and tarragon to the stock. Reduce until it has thickened, and add 1 teaspoon English mustard and a little of the thick béchamel or cream sauce to it. Boil the sauce for 2–5 minutes. Whisk in ¼ cup/ 60 g butter. Pour enough sauce into the two halves of the shell to lightly coat the shells. Add the lobster meat to the shells and pour the remainder of the sauce onto the meat. Then top with 2 tablespoons grated Parmesan cheese and 2 tablespoons melted butter, and brown briefly in a preheated oven at 240°C (475°F).

For an easier version, the lobster can be cut in half and broiled. Empty the two halves of the shell, coat them with a little cream sauce seasoned with 1 teaspoon English mustard (see cream sauce recipe above). Fill them with the sliced lobster flesh, cover with the same sauce and brown in the oven. Serve the lobster immediately.

Select Bibliography

Bayer, Robert and Juanita, *Lobsters Inside-Out: A Guide to the Maine Lobster* (Bar Harbor, ME, 1989)

Clifford, Harold B., *Charlie York: Maine Coast Fisherman* (Camden, ME, 1974)

Colquhoun, Kate, *Taste: The Story of Britain Through its Cooking* (New York, 2007)

Corson, Trevor, *The Secret Life of Lobsters* (New York, 2004)

Cowan, Diane F., 'Robbing the Lobster Cradle', *New York Times* (2006)

Davidson, Alan, *North Atlantic Seafood* (New York, 1979)

—, *Mediterranean Seafood* (Berkeley, CA, 2002)

—, *Seafood of South-East Asia* (Berkeley, CA, 2003)

—, *The Oxford Companion to Food* (New York, 2006)

Dueland, Joy V., *The Book of the Lobster* (Somersworth, NH, 1973)

Elwood, R. L., 'Pain Experience in Hermit Crabs', *British Journal of Animal Behaviour*, LXXVII/5 (May 2009), pp. 1243–6

Factor, Jan Robert, ed., *Biology of the Lobster: Homarus americanus* (San Diego, CA, 1995)

Gray, Howard, *The Western Rock Lobster: Panulirus cygnus* (Geraldton, Australia, 1992 and 1999), *Book 1: A Natural History*; and *Book 2: A History of the Fishery*

Gregory, Neville, and T. E. Lowe, 'A Humane End for Lobsters', *New Zealand Science Monthly* (Christchurch, New Zealand, 1999)

Handwerk, Brian, 'Lobsters Navigate by Magnetism, Study
    Says', *National Geographic News* (Washington, DC, 2003)
Herrick, Francis H., *Natural History of the American Lobster*
    (Washington, DC, 1911)
Hillman, Howard, *The New Kitchen Science* (Boston, MA, 2003)
Josselyn, John, *John Josselyn, Colonial Traveler: A Critical Edition of
    'Two Voyages to New England'* (Hanover, NH, 1988)
Larousse Gastronomique (New York, 2001)
'Lobsters: An International Dispute as to Whether They Are
    Fishes', *New York Times* (1902)
Montagné, Prosper, *Larousse Gastronomique* (New York, 2001)
Nicosia, Frank and Kari Lavalli, *Homarid Lobster Hatcheries: Their
    History and Role in Research, Management, and Aquaculture*
    (Seattle, WA, 1999)
Oliver, Sandra L., *Saltwater Foodways: New Englanders and Their Food,
    at Sea and Ashore, in the Nineteenth Century* (Mystic, CT, 1995)
Phillips, B. F. and J. Kittaka, *Spiny Lobsters: Fisheries and Culture*
    (London, 2000)
Phillips, Bruce F., *Lobsters: Biology, Management, Aquaculture and
    Fisheries* (Oxford and Ames, IA, 2006)
Prudden, T. M., *About Lobsters* (Freeport, ME, 1962)
Renfrew, Jane, *Food and Cooking in Prehistoric Britain* (London, 1985)
Sandler, Bea, *The African Cookbook* (Cleveland, OH, 1970)
Simonds, Nina, *Classic Chinese Cuisine* (Shelburne, VT, 1994)
Stavely, Keith and Kathleen Fitzgerald, *America's Founding Food*
    (Chapel Hill, NC, and London, 2004)
Stein, Rick, *Rick Stein's Complete Seafood* (Berkeley, CA, and
    Toronto, 2008)
Thomas, Lately, *Delmonico's: A Century of Splendor* (Boston, MA,
    1967)
van Wyk, Magdaleen, *The Complete South African Cookbook* (Cape
    Town, 2007)
Wheaton, Barbara Ketcham, *Savoring the Past: The French Kitchen
    and Table from 1300 to 1789* (New York, 1983)
White, Jasper, *Lobster at Home* (New York, 1998)
Wilson, Anne C., *Food and Drink in Britain: From the Stone Age to
    the 19th Century* (Chicago, IL, 1991)

Websites and Associations

Cooking

Trevor Corson: http://www.trevorcorson.tumblr.com/post/
    262203493/how-to-cook-a-lobster-humanely
Lobster Institute: http://www.lobsterinstitute.org
Royal Society for the Prevention of Cruelty to Animals
    (Australia): www.rspca.org.au
Rick Stein: www.rickstein.com
Jasper White: www.summershackrestaurant.com

Restaurants and Products

Clearwater Seafoods Limited Partnership: www.clearwater.ca
Crustastun: www.crustastun.com
Norsk Hummer AS: www.norskhummer.no
Shucks Maine Lobster: www.shucksmaine.com
Red Lobster Restaurants: www.redlobster.com

Sustainability

Blue Ocean Institute's Guide to Ocean Friendly Seafood:
www.blueocean.org

Environmental Defense Fund's Pocket Seafood Selector:
www.edf.org
Institute of Marine Research: www.imr.no/en
Lobster Institute: www.lobsterinstitute.org/index.php?page=121
Lobster conservancy: www.lobsters.org
Marine Stewardship Council: www.msc.org
Monterey Bay Aquarium's Seafood Watch Pocket Guide:
www.montereybayaquarium.org
Save Our Seas Foundation: www.saveourseas.com/projects/
lobsters_UK

Other Sites

US FDA Seafood Complete List 2008:http://www.accessdata.fda.
gov/scripts/SEARCH_SEAFOOD/index.cfm?other=complete
Marine lobsters: http://nlbif.eti.uva.nl/bis/lobsters.php
The Lobster Newsletter: www.fish.wa.gov.au/the_lobster_
newsletter/Index.html

Acknowledgements

I am grateful to the many people who provided information; the friends and lobster lovers who guided me through this project. Writing a book like this is impossible without the help of others. My thanks to all the people who made it possible including those unnamed.

I want to thank sincerely Lisa Townsend, Linda Forrest, Warren Holmes, Lois Wasoff and my book buddy, Suzanne Lowe. I thank Fran Grigsby, Katharine and John Esty, Anne and Richard Fortier, John Lowe, Adam, Eric, Laurie and Robin Van Loon and Ann Willard. I appreciate my writer's group support and feedback. Thanks to Carolyn Shohet for her wonderful help with the recipes. I owe special thanks to the extraordinary reference librarians at the Boston Public Library, Concord Public Library and Scheslinger Library.

I am particularly appreciative of those scientists and scholars for their advice including Dr Jelle Atema, Dr Robert Bayer, Dr Brian F. Beal, Dr Ernie Chang, Dr Diane Cowan, Dr Phil James, Dr John Booth, Howard Gray, Dr Neville Gregory, Dr Kari Lavalli, Larry Lovell, Dr Hirokazu Matsuda, Dr Sheila Patek, Dr Dorie Reents-Budet and Dr Susan Waddy. Thanks to Kathleen Wall, colonial foodways culinarian at Plimoth Plantation, and Kathleen Curtin, food historian, for their insights about the Pilgrims. Not to mention Trevor Corson, author of *The Secret Life of Lobsters*.

Thanks to Barbara Haber and Andy Smith – for my start in culinary history, and to culinary historians Elizabeth Gawthrop

Riely, Sandra L. Oliver and Barbara Ketcham Wheaton. I have enjoyed support from Grace Butler, Randy Testa, Kathi Twomey Wahed and many others.

For help with the many fisheries, I thank Elsa Sabas, Michael Campbell, Martin Mallet, Ron Cormier, Ann-Lisbeth Agnalt, Heidi Bray, Kelly Woods, Katie Chilles, Howard Gray, Maree Finnegan, Robert Curtotti. Several people from PETA, RSPCA and Shellfish Network offered help. Thanks to the Lobster Institute, the Maine Lobster Promotion Council and the Marine Stewardship Council.

I couldn't have done it without Mary Jo Alexander, Karen Carlson, Peter Faust and Jeff Robichaud. And, of course, my daily companions Riley and Reny.

Thanks to Cleo Townsend, my mom, who fed me my first lobster tail and taught me about good food.

Finally, I am indescribably grateful to my husband Jeff Greene for his inexhaustible support and sage advice.

Photo Acknowledgements

The author and publishers wish to express their thanks to the below sources of illustrative material and/or permission to reproduce it. (Some information not given in the captions is also given below.)

Photo Brooklyn Museum, NY: p. 55; photo Jane Burton/Warren Photographic, http://www.warrenphotographic.co.uk: p. 16; © cbpix/Shutterstock.com 2009: p. 74; Images © Clearwater: pp. 76, 77; © Paul Cowan/2010 iStock International Inc.. p. 59; photos © Greg Currier Photography of Camden, Maine: pp. 10, 106; photo courtesy Everett Collection/Rex Features: p. 64; © evgenyb/2010 iStock International Inc.: p. 85; photo Patrick Frilet/Rex Features: p. 50; gmnicholas/2010 iStock International Inc.: p. 53; photo courtesy Goldmark Gallery: p. 62; © FutoshiHamaguchi/2010 iStock International Inc.: p. 71; courtesy joerivanveen/2010 iStock International Inc.: p. 14; © Junker/Shutterstock.com 2009: pp. 92–3; photos Library of Congress, Washington, DC: pp. 21, 66; photo © Jamie MacMillan: p. 56; photo courtesy Marine Stewardship Council (msc.org): p. 113; photo © Ivan Massar: pp. 88, 89, 105; photos Vetle Misje: pp. 104, 108; photo Jeff Mullins © ReefWreckand-Critter.com: p. 20; Museum of Fine Arts, Boston (photo © 2010 Museum of Fine Arts, Boston): p. 26; photo © Mystic Seaport Collection, Mystic, CT ~ www.mysticseaport.org: p. 37; © neelsky/Shutterstock.com 2009: p. 11; National Gallery, London: p. 29; photo ND/Roger-Viollet/Rex Features: p. 48; photos provided by

Index

italic numbers refer to illustrations; **bold** to recipes